Living Healthy

6 simple strategies to achieve a healthy life
physically, spiritually, and financially

By Erick O. Bell, CPA

Living Healthy: 6 simple strategies to achieve a healthy life physically, spiritually, and financially

Erick O. Bell, CPA

© 2021 Erick O. Bell

Scripture quotations are taken from the Holy Bible, New International Version

This book is dedicated to my four amazing children, Kasani, Mekhi, Lucas, and Benjamin. I wrote this book with each of you in mind in hopes that when I am no longer able to tell you stories you can tell them to yourselves through these words.

Prologue

This book has been over a decade in the making. There are six simple strategies I live by to promote a healthy spiritual relationship, stay in a healthy physical condition, and manage a healthy financial position.

Let's first set expectations. Throughout this entire book I use the term 'healthy' as a proxy for the following words: 'happiness', 'success', 'contentment', 'peace', 'prosperity'. Essentially, healthy is all those things we wish for our lives and our family regardless of our ethnicity, religion, political orientation, sexual orientation, income level, social upbringing or childhood trauma.

I make the illogical connection between turning 30 years old and stepping into my true purpose for life. It was about the age of 30, when I started examining what truly made me happy and how I could achieve it. I began scouring my life experiences and related lessons and landed on six relatively simple strategies to achieve my zen:

1. Do it First
2. Forgive Yourself
3. Be Consistent
4. Reduce Distractions
5. Start Small and Gradually Increase
6. Educate Yourself

There is nothing new under the sun. If it is true, it is not new. If you are hearing it new, it's probably not true. Unless you have been intentionally not reading books, listening to elders or friends, avoiding the internet at all costs, and basically living under a rock that has been wedged in between a canyon gorge...you have heard these six strategies in some form or another. The pages that follow will not give you new information. You have heard all of this before, but perhaps you have not yet started implementing some (or all) of the strategies yet.

There is a difference between knowing, understanding, and executing. The intention of this book is not to tackle the 'knowing'. This is information you have already absorbed, and quite possibly acquired over a series of formal and informal conversations. My goal with this book is to increase your understanding of these strategies by challenging you to examine how these strategies have been or can be manifested in your life. This is the process of moving from knowledge to understanding – from acquiring information to explaining and examining what you know. My hope is this book will inspire you to increase your execution of these strategies. Each chapter concludes with practical steps you can implement to incorporate these strategies as a natural extension of your person.

Caution – this book will not work for everyone. If you are looking for quick fixes to your life problems, this book will entertain, but not lead to systemic change in your life. If you are still unclear about your life goals and how you are choosing to define 'healthy', this book will point towards some different directions but it will not propel you in any specific direction. For those who are clear in their definition of success, and ready for a subtly dramatic change in your life and results then you are between the right book covers.

As you navigate through this book you will learn more about my life's choices, my successes and failures, and the many hats I have worn (and still wear) in my professional, philanthropical, and professional careers. One of those hats is serving as the chairman and executive director for a non-profit organization that provides summer camps for high school students interested in learning more about careers in accounting and finance. Each year, I am given the honor of welcoming students and parents during the orientation of our annual summer program. I tend to repeat the same general motivational speech, adding voice inflections to emphasize excitement, sincerity, folly, and professionalism. I always end my schtick by presenting a riddle:

> *"Three frogs are sitting on a rock along the riverbed. It is a warm day and the breeze is not blowing at its usual pace, creating a more than usual level of discomfort for each frog. One frog declares he has had enough and decides to jump off the rock. How many frogs are left on the rock?"*

After taking a few wrong answers, I reveal the correct answer: 3 frogs. I then explain to the students there is a difference from deciding to do something and actually doing something. So before we launch into the meat and potatoes of this book I present you with this challenge: don't just *decide* to jump, but instead take action and *jump*!

Do it first

Breakfast is the most important meal of the day. Pay yourself first. Seek ye first the Kingdom of God. This is not a novel concept to do the things that are most important first. Despite hearing these mantras for the first 25 years of my life, it did not really stick until I read Stephen Covey's book, *The 7 Habits of Highly Successful People* and his story about "big rocks first". Here is the strategy in a condensed format:

> *Imagine you have a bucket, which you are trying to fill with rocks, pebbles, and sand. How do you get everything in the bucket? If you put the sand in first, you leave no room for rocks and pebbles. If you put the pebbles in first, you might have room for the sand, but the rocks won't fit. The only way to fit everything in the bucket is to put the big rocks in first, then the pebbles. Then, you can pour the sand into the bucket and it will fill all the spaces in between.*

The first strategy in living a healthy lifestyle is identifying those things that are the most important and tackling them first. The more you can automate this task, the better. The more you disdain this task, the more critical it is that you do it first. This is really about prioritizing what really matters in your life and demonstrating those priorities in your actions.

Forgive yourself

I do not know where I first saw this image below. Maybe it was at a self-empowerment workshop at a business conference, maybe I read it in a book, or maybe it was a picture in someone's office.

Although I do not know when I first saw this image, I am pretty sure it did not resonate with me then as it does now. For those who have tasted success, this is a great illustration of how complicated the path towards success can be and how many failures are sprinkled along the

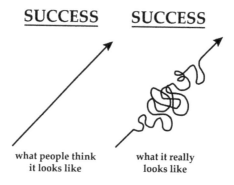

SUCCESS   SUCCESS

what people think   what it really
it looks like   looks like

path. Without a clear understanding of your ultimate goal and an abundance of grace for yourself, you will never reach life's satisfaction. We have to accept that we will not be perfect, we will let others down and let ourselves down. Nevertheless, we have to keep moving forward. The second strategy to living healthy is to forgive yourself; acknowledge our mistakes and forgive ourselves.

Be consistent

I have spoken to many students, mentees, and employees who directly reported to me who have shared with me their grand master plans for life. We have broached various subjects, from starting a new business, continuing their formal education, buying their dream house, or traveling to a new destination. I have also seen not much come from those plans. Man, that sounds harsh but it is true because what matters is not the plan but the commitment to consistency in executing that plan.

We are products of what we do the most often. When I see someone thriving in business, art, or family. I know this to be the result of consistency. I had the honor of being able to visit the Sistine Chapel in Vatican City. When I entered the chapel I stood among a crowd of hundreds and stared at the work of art on the ceiling. It took Michelangelo 4 years to paint this piece. Moreover, he did not even want to paint the ceiling. He initially balked at the request from Pope Julius II because he was working on a marble tomb and considered himself a sculptor rather than a painter. Michelangelo also found working on the Sistine Chapel to be unpleasant since he painted the ceiling in a standing position reaching above his head. He even wrote a poem about his misery. Nevertheless, he was consistent in his work for four years.

The third strategy to living a healthy life is to be consistent, even when the work is less desirable and sometimes downright painful.

Reduce distractions

It really does not matter what your goals are, there will always be barriers preventing you from achieving them. Some of those barriers are systemic (racial, economic, education, gender, etc.) These types of barriers require the heavy lifting and support of our broader community to operate alongside our individual efforts to effect change and make an impact. I have experienced some tremendous strides in breaking these barriers that I will save for a different discussion. There are other barriers to our goals which are self-imposed. For example, negative 'friendships', bouts of self-doubt, lethargy, unproductive habits, etc.

There will always be distractions in our path, and we have to be resilient and responsible enough to acknowledge them and move past them. I hear students complain about the distractions they have all the time when reading textbooks and completing homework assignments. I always respond with an analogy about my commute to the college campus. I live approximately 30 miles from three campus. My commute requires me to drive along three different freeways to get from home to work; thankfully it is all opposite commute traffic. On my 30 mile commute I am only interested in four road signs: the sign to the first freeway entrance, the sign to the second freeway connector, the sign to the third freeway connector, and the sign to exit to my campus. I then ask the students to commiserate with me and my disgust with how many unnecessary signs are on the roads for my commute. There are speed limit signs, merging signs, signs indicating gas stations and food, signs announcing a different city and (what I know to be outdated) population sizes, and of course, signs for about 20 exits that I am not interested in.

Of course, the students give me the strange look which is my opening to remind them that distractions are always there. But when we know what our goal is, we can block out the distractions and focus on our personalized road map.

Start small and gradually increase

Dream Big! This strategy is not about having small dreams, it is about taking intentional steps to reach big dreams. I started writing this book with the expectation it will become a New York Times Bestseller. (Why would I expect anything less?) In order to achieve this status, the book needs to have at least 5,000-10,000 copies sold in a week, and those sales have to be from diverse sources (bookstores, websites, etc.). This is clearly not an easy feat to achieve. It requires an impressive number of existing followers, strong marketing media platforms, and a few convincing endorsements from celebrities. Let's see – to date, I have no celebrities endorsing this book, no publishing company promoting the book months before its release date, and I have a combined 20 followers across my few incognito social media accounts (at the time of this writing I have no social media accounts in my name).

The key word in this strategy is 'start'. Even if the first step is small, you have to start. Without writing a manuscript, I had zero chances of securing a publishing company. Without self-publishing this book, there would be zero pathways of getting these ideas into the hands of the person who knows the person who knows the influential celebrity. Without researching how to increase book sales, I would never seriously entertain creating an intentional social media presence dedicated to helping people achieve a healthy lifestyle.

Everyone loves a rags to riches, humble beginning story. To reach that healthy lifestyle, you have to start somewhere. And it does not have to be a grand gesture, just do something.

Educate yourself

Knowledge is key! Do I need to say more? Well I will, but first let me acknowledge a few things. I would not have launched my career in accounting or earned my certification as a public accountant without earning a bachelor's degree. I also would not have this amazing opportunity to be a tenured college professor – which by the way is currently my largest single source of income –

without earning a master's degree. Here comes the shocker...College does not make you smarter. A college degree is not synonymous with education.

The quest for knowledge is ingrained in a human being. It is the pathway for self-improvement and can only be achieved when a person is curious enough to find ways and means to dig deeper and explore further. I do not begrudge formal education, it is an absolute necessity to the three branches of learning – reading, writing, and arithmetic. But seriously, you can learn enough by the 8th grade to survive in this society. Delving deeper into your history, the logic behind math, comprehension of information, and the basic tenets of researching are sufficiently covered by the time you earn your high school diploma. Once you decide on a career, college becomes more important because you can more intimately explore accounting or psychology or biology. You are also improving on those basic skills you learned in high school. By the time you earn a college degree, you are more than functioning in society – you have the ability to control society (if you choose). Masters and PhD degrees are just showing off.

But educating yourself is not found in degrees or accomplishments. It is the result of a deep curiosity or unquenched thirst for understanding. Education is really knowledge, and knowledge can be found in intuition, research, authorities, books, habits, rationalism, and deadlines. In fact, I used a combination of all these things (plus my diploma and degrees) to pen the following pages. I will talk about a lot of things in this book – and I challenge you, I encourage you, I employ you to take the next step and educate yourself on those things that truly pique your interests.

PART I

LIVING
PHYSICALL
Y
HEALTHY

Chapter 1 – Do it first...Physically

In the morning you hear my voice; in the morning I lay my request before you and wait expectantly.
- Psalms 5:3

What does your first hour of the morning look like? Here is my routine: wake up, reach for my cellphone to see what messages I received, catch myself before I enter my phone's passcode, reach for my tablet instead and read the news. First local news, then national news from a "liberal outlet" and national news from a "conservative outlet". I like to stay level-headed so I aim to hear both sides of every story.

Listen, I have two toddlers in the house, and I know if I don't read the news before they wake up then I will miss the opportunity to read the news at all during the day. I also know that what I do first thing in the morning will dictate my day.

My other morning routine is to get out and go for a 3 mile run or long walk. I know if I don't get my exercise within the first hour, chances are it won't get done.

Within the first hour of each day, find a way to get 15-30 minutes of exercise.

My unflattering Wii character

In November 2012 I became obsessed with finding a Nintendo Wii. I visited an amusement park with my older son and we spent about one hour in a tent playing a tennis video game on a new console, the Nintendo Wii. I decided within that hour I "needed" to have one. I did not realize how difficult it would be to find a Wii. For the next three days, I visited about five stores and called around eight other stores before I found a GameStop that had a small inventory about 30 miles east of my house. I immediately jumped in my car to purchase the console, and quickly returned home to set up my Wii. Thankfully, there were no sheriffs on the stretch of the highway I was speeding on. The console is not worth a $500 speeding ticket, but that day I would have probably thought differently. I spent that entire evening playing tennis with myself working up a good sweat.

I am not a video gamer. This was my first (and last) video console since the original Nintendo NES in 1990 when I was in high school. (I am referring to the Super Mario Bros. and Legend of Zelda days; plus it was my older brother's gaming system, not mine). I forgot game consoles only come with one or two games, so I was enticed to buy more games. I bought boxing, golf, baseball, Karaoke. Then I was enticed to buy a wheel to hold the controller for my racing car game, then I bought a guitar to hold the controller for my Guitar Hero game. Eventually, I was coerced into buying a Wii Fit, a pad that you place on the floor to measure your weight, test your balance, evaluate your agility, and shame you!

The game allowed you to make a Wii character where you can manipulate the hair, skin color, eye color, clothes, etc. The one attribute you could not manipulate was the weight. My son created his Wii, it was cute and looked like him. My then fiancé (now wife) created her Wii, it was pretty, just like her. I created my Wii and his belly was slightly sticking out of his shirt. (My belly does not stick outside of my shirt). The Wii no longer was my favorite pastime. It reminded me that I was overweight for my height.

I became obsessed with getting my Wii character to better reflect how I wanted it to look. Each day I would wake up in the morning and complete a 20 minute workout routine. I was motivated to stop letting my son and fiancé get laughs at my expense every time we fired up the game console.

Emmett v. Clinton

The first time I was eligible to vote in a presidential election was in 1992 and I casted my vote for Bill Clinton. He had my vote for two reasons – one, my mom was voting for him and two, his saxophone performance on the Arsenio Hall show. This is a sad testament, but unfortunately this is very common. As Americans, we generally do not put the thought necessary into electing our leader who has the authority to bring our country to war, enact executive orders, and influence global relations.

I followed President Bill Clinton's career over the next eight years: his economic expansion, low unemployment, Family and Medical Leave Act, paying down $360 billion in government debt, and appointing the most diverse Cabinet in American history at the time. He also had a few disappointments: doubled the number of prisoners through his 1994 Crime Bill, his compromised "don't ask, don't tell" policy, failure to regulate the financial services market, and of course... Monica Lewinsky. Despite his

15

highs and lows, I still have vivid memories of seeing Bill Clinton wearing his white hat, matching his pale white legs while wearing shorts that barely peered below his baggy t-shirt. He also had a swarm of secret service agents running with him – including Dan Emmett.

In 2012, Emmet released a book titled "*Within Arm's Length: The Extraordinary Life and Career of a Special Agent in the United States Secret Service*". In the book, Emmett explains why President Clinton's jogging was so unpopular among the Secret Service agents assigned to protect him. Emmett and his fellow agents attempted to talk Clinton out of running in unsecured areas, including having a quarter-mile track installed along the perimeter of the White House grounds. Clinton did not like the running track though, he remained committed to his morning jogs because they served as a temporary mental escape from the White House.

Clinton did not prioritize running to simply keep pounds off, he also considered it a way to connect with voters. Random runners would constantly want to join the President on his run, and Clinton would obviously oblige.

President Clinton jogged about three days a week, for about 30 minutes and Emmett recalls it being a challenge to find Secret Service agents who could cover the job with the President, while carrying a weapon and radio and remaining alert enough to respond to any potential dangers.

Clinton won the battle and continued his morning jogs, serving as an example to all Americans. It is actually surprising there were so many deflectors during that time criticizing Clinton for his morning running routine. Fewer than 10 percent of Americans exercise daily, even though exercise is the best thing anyone can do for his or her health. Scientists believe death rates could be reduced by 9% in men and 15% in women if unfit people became fit.

Emmett noted that the Secret Service eventually mapped out a few running routes that satisfied both their security requirements and the President's request. Clinton would run the dirt trail on the National Mall, along the reflecting pool at the Lincoln Memorial and along the Potomac. To this day, whenever I visit Washington D.C. and can stay in a hotel near the National Mall I recreate that same morning routine.

Science backs this up

There are proven benefits to working out in the morning instead of the evening. I will share five of them with you. One benefit is really obvious and we don't need a scientist to prove it: there are fewer distractions. This is before your day gets started, no one is competing for the TV or your time. There are no calls, messages, or emails to distract you. When you wait until the end of the day to perform our workout routine, you are subjecting yourself to the 4:55pm call from your boss with an urgent request, the fatigue from the day's stresses, the "can't miss" after work drinks with colleagues, or the big game that starts at 6:30pm. There are just too many distractions as the day drags along.

Another (more scientific) benefit is a morning workout matches your body's hormonal fluctuations. Your cortisol levels typically increase in the morning and drop in the evening. Cortisol is a hormone that keeps you awake and alert. Your cortisol levels typically peaks at 8am. Low levels of cortisol can cause weakness, fatigue, and low blood pressure.

A third scientific benefit is exercise helps regulate your appetite by reducing gherlin, the hunger hormone. A study published in Medicine and Science in Sports and Exercise had 35 women walk on a treadmill for 45 minutes in the morning. Next, researchers measured the women's brain waves as they viewed photos of flowers and food. A week later, the process was repeated without morning exercise. The researchers found that the women's brains had a stronger response to food photos when they did not exercise in the morning. This study posited that morning workouts improve how your brain responds to food cues. But I don't need a study to reach this conclusion.

I notice when I exercise in the morning I am more cautious about what I eat (at least through the first half of the day) because I am cautious not to waste my efforts in the morning with an unhealthy breakfast comprised of a sugary donut, greasy sausage biscuit, or overly sweetened hot beverage.

A fourth benefit is an overall improvement of your mood. Physical activity is a natural remedy for stress. During exercise, your brain makes more endorphins, the 'happy' neurotransmitters behind a runner's high. It also works as a distraction to anxious thoughts. A morning exercise gives you a sense of accomplishment leading to an optimistic outlook for the day – what a great way to start your day.

A fifth benefit is better sleep. A study in the Vascular Health and Risk Management demonstrated adults got better sleep on the days they exercised at 7am. After the morning workout, the participants spent more time in deep sleep and experienced fewer nighttime awakenings.

(An added sixth benefit is a natural increase in your melatonin levels from working outside in the morning. Light exposure early in the day help increase melatonin levels at night. Melatonin is a hormone that relaxes the body, leading to sleep. Lower levels of melatonin secretion in the autumn-winter period can increase appetite and lead to weight gain.)

Chapter 2 – Forgive yourself...
Physically

*Brothers and sisters I do not consider myself yet to have taken hold of it.
But one thing I do: Forgetting what is behind and straining toward what
is ahead...*
- Philippians 3:13

n 2015, I convinced myself to run a half-marathon.
Let me explain. In 2014, I had reached the point in
my career at the large accounting firm where it was
no longer just about my ability to reconcile t-accounts and
analyze financial statements, but rather my ability to sell
accounting services to clients. I had hit a wall in my
career path and was stretching myself outside of my
comfort zone to become a 'rainmaker'. I spent an
enormous amount of time strategizing on how to bring
new clients to the firm willing to spend anywhere between
$200,000-$1,000,000 for each engagement. I was on a
team of 12 people across the Northwest region who were
developing the firm's relationship with a large company
that sold athletic gear. This apparel company was hosting
a weekend of competitive activities in Oregon. I was asked
to be one of the six people to represent the firm during
this competitive weekend. I agreed.

The weekend included a ropes challenge, bungee
jumping, ziplining, geocaching, 10 mile runs, obstacle
courses, bike races and relay races. We stayed in cabins
on site that had about 8 bunkbeds in each room. By the
time we arrived, there were few beds left and I sheepishly
climbed up to a top bunk near the door. I had to leave my
duffel bag on the bed, because the rooms did not have

closets or dressers. We ate breakfast, lunch, and dinner on site with all the other participants at the same time each day. Honestly, it felt like I was in a reform camp for troubled teens. At night, we would sit around bonfires with our client, and other teams participating, and sing songs I had never heard before. Apparently, everyone knew the words of the songs except me. I was truly out of my element.

Here is the thing: I was out of shape when I agreed to be one of the six team members who would compete in this weekend-long event. I can't say I was ever 'in shape', but when I was younger I had a strong metabolism. Back then I could wolf down a fast food combo and then play basketball for two hours at a high energy level. But I was not young anymore, and the thought of running 3 miles made me question if I was signing a death sentence by agreeing to go. (Side story, I did have a near-death experience that weekend when I took a wrong turn, fell over a cliff, and then got lost in the mountains. At one point, I wanted to just stop moving and wait for the helicopter to come find me – yes, there was a rescue helicopter and paramedic on site. Thankfully, I did not die. I ended up walking to the other side of the mountain that led to a trail to put me back with my team).

I resolved to get in some semblance of shape before the weekend. My goal was to complete a 3 mile run during the event. I did complete the 3 mile run that weekend, and also an obstacle course and ropes challenge that lead to a 'leap of faith' from a telephone pole to a trapeze bar suspended 80 feet in the air. Our team did not win the competition, in fact, we did not even come close. We did manage to strengthen the relationship with our potential client, which was our ultimate goal anyway.

So this is why I decided to run a half-marathon in 2015. In the process of preparing for this weekend challenge, I had caught the bug of becoming healthy again. I realized the mental benefits of running early in the morning (See Chapter 1) and the physical benefits of eating more carefully. I felt the next logical step was to challenge myself from 3 miles to 13.2 miles. And now that I have written this, I realize that was not a very logical thought process.

Even if you miss a day or cannot hit your goal, forgive yourself and move on to the next day or the next goal.

Best laid plans often go awry

My first priority was to find a half marathon. I decided on the Disney half marathon, which zigzagged through both Disneyland and California Adventure before weaving through the streets of Anaheim, California. The race included running through the Anaheim Angels baseball stadium before heading back towards the finish line at the Disney complex. I love Disneyland – it reminds me of my childhood and the nostalgia of family vacations. The race included meet and greets with Disney characters scattered around the 13.2 miles. I was sold! The problem was that the race was happening in 12 weeks.

I researched how to prepare for a half marathon in 12 weeks. This is what the plan generally looks like:
- Run four days a week, rest three days a week
- Increase your total miles each week from 9 miles to 20 miles

- The longest runs are on Sundays, starting with 4 miles and peaking at 10 miles
- The shortest runs are Tuesdays at 2 miles
- During the week, the runs get longer and more challenging - incorporating hill running and interval running.

On day 1, I had a plan for the next 84 days to get me to race day. Day 1, I nailed it. It was a rest day. Day 2, of course I handled it – a manageable 2 mile run. Days 3-6 included one 3 mile run and two rest days. I've already knew I could run 3 miles, and surely I was a master at resting. Day 7 was the one I was looking forward to - a 4 mile run. I checked it off, and at that moment I knew that I could handle the next 77 days.

Somewhere in week 2 - I got a bit behind. No worries, I could swap some rest days. Week 3 – I am thinking "I don't have to follow the plan exactly". Week 4 – I am wondering if I should ask for a refund for the $120 race entry fee. I realized it was harder than I anticipated to stay on track for 12 straight weeks.

Perfect does not exist

Perfect is the enemy of good. This quote is usually attributed to Voltaire. He actually wrote "best is the enemy of the good" (*il meglio e nemico del bene*) and cited it as an old Italian proverb in 1770. Voltaire was explaining that while a concept of "the best" exists, "good" will never be good enough. I tend to agree. I would rather coach the best basketball team, than a good basketball team. I would rather eat a perfect burger, instead of a good burger. Our society suffers from this habit of perfectionism. I have seen it in corporate America with colleagues, I have seen it in classrooms with students, I have seen it at the kitchen table with my kids completing their homework. This habit of perfection can hurt you and lead to unhappiness. We end up spending more time on tasks; we cannot define what our ultimate goal is because we are seeking to attain something that is essentially unattainable. Those who have worked with me will attest, I always work hard and I always give my very best. I want to give more than I actually have to give - so understand when I say this – *perfection does not exist.*

We have to learn to be comfortable with the "Golden Mean". The golden mean or golden middle way is the desirable middle between two extremes, one of excess and the other of deficiency. One of the earliest illustrations of this idea in modern pop culture is probably in the mythological Cretan tale of Icarus. Icarus' father, Daedalus built feathered wings for himself and Icarus so they could escape the clutches of King Minos. Daedalus warned his ambitious son whom he loved to "fly the middle course", between the sea spray and the sun's heat. Icarus did not heed his father; he flew up and up until the sun melted the wax from his wings. Icarus fell into the sea and drowned.

The Eudemian Ethics is a work of philosophy by Aristotle. Aristotle provided an example of the golden mean in action: courage is a virtue, but taken to excess would manifest itself as reckless, and in deficiency, it would be considered cowardice. The key is to find a middle ground that leans toward perfection, not deficiency, while acknowledging we may never achieve perfection.

Sure I struggled to get through weeks 6 and 7 of the half marathon training plan. But I forgave myself, I acknowledged that I was not perfect but I was able to run 7 miles without stopping and I was making progress. I was not an 'out-of-shape' slob and I did not have a six-pack of abs with tennis ball calf muscles. I was not on either extreme, I was in the 'golden mean'.

Forgiveness strategies

Moving beyond this desire for perfection is not a short trip around the corner. It takes time. First, set short, achievable goals and allow yourself time for reflection. When I decided to write this book (the third time) I aimed to write one imperfect chapter each night, hopefully finishing 3-4 chapters each week. Note, I was not looking for a well-written chapter but something on paper. I knew my second step would be to reread everything in chunks and edit/rewrite/research/clarify.

Second, celebrate the process not the product. I will never forget my CPA exam experience and the best advice I received on the night I finished the fourth exam. I decided to schedule my exam about 2 hours away from home because I wanted to limit distractions. I asked a friend if I could stay at her place for the time I was scheduled to take this 2-day, 17 hour exam. She was not a CPA, not an accountant, not even a business major. She had no idea why I was subjecting myself to this behemoth exam, but she knew it was important to me and that I had sacrificed a lot to do well on the exam. After the second day, I returned back to her apartment. She presented me with a cake she had bought that said "congratulations". I asked why she congratulating me I didn't know if I passed the exams. I explained to her that the pass rate for the CPA exam is 50%. She said "I am not congratulating you on passing the exam, I am congratulating you for going through the process." From that day on, I have always focused on celebrating the process, not the outcome. I can control the process – not the outcome.

Third, put the appropriate importance on this task. I had to ask myself what was the worst thing that could happen if I did not run the entire 13.2 miles or even complete the half-marathon? Well, I could always walk a few miles. Even if I decided to not participate in the race, I would walk away with being able to run 7 miles continuously. (Maybe 9 miles if I got back to the routine).

I was able to get back on track. Around week 8, I was supposed to run a 10k race - I did that without all my required training and really enjoyed myself. It was the catalyst I needed to keep going. I finished the half-marathon in Anaheim. It was so much fun. I set a goal of finishing under 2 hours, and ended up finishing with 2:00:39. I did not meet that goal but I enjoyed it so much. I have completed five half marathons since, Las Vegas, Oakland, and Disneyland a few more times.

Chapter 3 – Be consistent...Physically

Therefore, my dear brothers and sisters, stand firm. Let nothing move you. Always give yourself fully to the work of the Lord, because you know that your labor in the Lord is not in vain.
- 1 Corinthians 15:58

nvy can be quite the motivator! Many years ago I was pursuing a young lady who had previously dated an ex-NFL player. Let's just say I was not in NFL shape (let's be honest and say I was not in backyard-two-hand-touch football shape). In my mind, if I had any chance of being successful in my pursuit, I needed to get back in shape.

I am sure you have heard of the "freshmen fifteen". It references the 15 pounds a freshmen in college gains from eating in the dorm, drinking too much beer at college parties, sedentary lectures and study sessions, and generally not getting enough sleep. In accounting and law firms, we also have a "freshmen fifteen" phenomenon. The first year someone works at the firm, we are treated to fancy dinners (which always consist of appetizer, entree and dessert), drinking too much liquor at work parties (for every reason imaginable), sedentary work and meetings, and generally not getting enough sleep. I was a victim of the "freshmen fifteen" when I started working. I needed to get back in shape.

Have a normal routine that you follow on a monthly, weekly, or daily basis. Change the routine periodically to ensure that your body does not get 'used' to the workout.

Confession: I love routines

I am an accountant at heart, what else can I say. I love organization, structure, and routines. I set a plan to get back in shape. I signed up for a membership at a gym that had multiple locations. In my line of work, I was constantly traveling to different cities in the San Francisco Bay Area and I needed the flexibility to work out in the morning before visiting my clients.

The night before work, I would select and iron my clothes for the next day. I would put them on a hanger on my bedroom door and also pack a duffle bag with a cosmetic bag, towel, shower shoes, underwear, socks, and work shoes. I would also lay out my work-out clothes on the chair near my bed. Then I would map out where the nearest gym was in proximity to my client, and figure out how long it would take me to get to that gym. I knew it took me 8 minutes to wake up, put on my work-out clothes, brush my teeth, throw some water on my face and be out the door. This meant I was waking up sometime between 5:23am and 5:44am (I was very specific).

The next morning I would arrive at the gym and spend 20 minutes on the treadmill. Starting the first 2 minutes at 2:00, then increasing to 4:00, then up to 5:00, then to 6:00, then to 7:00 and ending at 8:00. Every 3 minutes I would increase intervals until I hit the maximum, and then gradually decrease. Next, I would go to free weights and do three sets of 15: curls, shoulder press, arm lifts. Then, I would go to a contraption that worked on abdominal muscles. Finally, I would go to the machines and work on legs: curls, extensions, and presses. After, I would go to the showers and dress for work. My routine at the gym took about 55-60 minutes, depending on whether I needed to wait for a machine or weight.

I was consistent. I did this four days a week, Monday through Thursday for six weeks. It did not matter where I was headed (San Ramon, Atherton, or Rohnert Park) – I found the nearest gym. It did not matter what time my first client meeting was - I adjusted my wake-up time to account for traffic and the occasional wait time at the gym. Results came quickly; I saw some immediate improvement in my weight and toning of my muscles.

Then I hit a wall. My body was used to the 20 minute treadmill, so it did not have the same impact. My muscles became comfortable with 25 pound dumbbells and needed more tension to grow. So I changed up my routine. It was still around 55-60 minutes in the gym, but I started using elliptical machines, and added swimming into the rotation. I created a schedule where I would focus on arms on Day 1, shoulders on Day 2, legs on Day 3, gut and abs on Day 4. After another 8 weeks of improvement, I hit another wall - so I changed my routine again.

Routines can be fun

People are creatures of habit. Think about the first thing you do when you walk into your house. You do it religiously without even thinking about it. Habit. The question is whether this is an intentional habit we set that benefits our lives or whether it is... just something that we do. My wife has a strange habit that she does whenever she is driving through a yellow light. She brings her hands to her lips, kisses them and then pushes her fingers into the air. When we first started dating I would watch her do that - and eventually I asked what was up with that gesture. She said when she was a teenager she wanted to speed through yellow lights and then would say a quick prayer that she didn't get caught. Uh, okay.

People who do not have any routines can suffer from stress, poor sleep, poor eating, ineffective use of time, and poor physical condition. No routine means you are always living in this world of worrying when it will all get done, playing 'catch-up', opting for quick dinners (i.e., fast food), and not making the most use of your time. Being consistent leads to improved mental health, allowing for time for relax and reduce stress anxiety. A consistent schedule also leads to more regular sleep patterns.

Consistency is challenging

Why is it so hard to be consistent? Why do so many people struggle with self-discipline? It's simple: We focus too much on the outcome, and not the process (See Chapter 2). Here is the truth, I never achieved ex-NFL physical prowess, and I did not find success in my pursuit of that lady either. My short term goal was to acquire ripped abs, toned arms and a slim waist. There was no way I was going to accomplish that with 4-6 weeks of 45 minute workout routines. However, like I pointed out – I like routines and I like structure.

I found out there were other benefits associated with waking up before the sun breaks and starting my day.

- Benefit 1 – I avoided the worse part of traffic. My client visits were about 30-45 miles from my home (in all directions), but it could easily take 1½ to 2 hours to get there in morning traffic. I was reducing my commute by more than one half by starting my day earlier.
- Benefit 2 – I had 30-40 minutes to reflect on my day and what I wanted to accomplish that day. I would reflect on the difficult conversations I needed to have and how I could start them. I would create a mental to-do list of priorities.
- Benefit 3 – I ate healthier that day. There was no way I was driving through a restaurant to order a high calorie, low nutritional biscuit sandwich slathered with butter and oozing with cheese.
- Benefit 4 – I did have some physical benefits from exercising. My waistline did decrease, my weight did go down, my arms got cut a little bit more. Nothing drastic to the outsider's perspective, but it was a huge boost to my confidence. My confidence impacted how I spoke in meetings, how I greeted people, and how I responded to criticism.

When I took the pressure off my intended outcome, and appreciated the process in the moment, it gave me a sense of clarity and purpose.

Slow consistency is better than inconsistency

Nearly all of us have heard the story of the Tortoise and the Hare, one of Aesop's Fables. The story concerns a rabbit who is making fun of a turtle for having a slow pace. The turtle gets perturbed with the rabbit's taunting and challenges him to a race. The rabbit's reaction is similar to any of our own reactions - hysterical laughing and finger pointing. All the animals in the woods gather around for this race – there isn't much in the way of entertainment in the woods that do not involve the Lion King's circle of life illustration of how animals are eaten by other animals.

At the start of the race, the rabbit shoots out down the path leaving the turtle to wipe the dust from her crooked mouth. The rabbit looks behind him and realizes this win was easier than he envisioned. He decides to enjoy a lunch, followed by an afternoon nap. While the rabbit slumbers, the turtle continues with her consistent pace and heads towards the finish line. The pace of the turtle is so slow, the crowd disperses so there is no cheering or jeering to disrupt the rabbit's peaceful rest. As the sun sets, the shadow covers the tree and the chilling wind wakes up the rabbit. The rabbit realizes he has overslept and now risks the chances of losing the race and his pride. He darts back onto the track, but it is too late. The turtle has crossed the finish line – she flashes her crooked smile and winks.

I think we are partial to this fable because it leaves us with two important lessons: (1) we have to put aside our self-presumptuous arrogance, and not assume the relative superiority or inferiority of a competitor and (2) slow, consistent and incremental progress can win the race. A little a day can add up to a much larger success later down the line.

Becoming more consistent

I can offer 4 strategies for becoming more consistent in your physical training (and in your life):

• Be fully engaged in the moment – understand your purpose and commit to the process. This means asking yourself, "what if I don't lose weight, will I still appreciate the process?" Quiet the noise that tends to waste mental, spiritual, and emotional energy. Don't worry about the past or the future – just live in the moment.

• Anticipate the dip – author Seth Godin noted anything worth pursuing will have a messy middle. Regardless of how well your plans are laid out, you will have a dip in energy, motivation, and drive. Push forward anyways. I did not wake up at 5:38 excited to go workout. (When I arrived at the gym 40 minutes later I was likely still grumbling). I knew it was a process and I knew consistency was the key, so I persevered even when I did not feel like it.

• Get back to the basics – I overextended myself on certain days. In my eagerness to push myself harder, I pushed myself too hard. I was discouraged, and would often say to myself *maybe I am not meant to be in better shape.* This is when I would employ one of my strategies from anticipating the dip – I would go back to the basics. I would just choose two or three days of treadmill work or free weights. I would reduce the pounds I lifted or the number of reps I completed. I would go back to the place where I had success and live there for a few days until my confidence was built back up. Remember the last places were you found success - so you can always turn back to them for security and confidence.

• Find an accountability partner – the benefits of a having a personal trainer is that she or he is your motivator. They are standing at the door waiting for you to come in the gym. They greet you with a "attaboy" and encourage you to get going. I find it interesting that we are more concerned about letting down others, then letting down ourselves. When we agree to meet someone at the shoreline for a jog or the bottom of the trail for a hike, then we are extra motivated to be on time, dressed and ready to go.

Create a workout routine that is realistic to you and achievable for you. If you are more energized during your lunch break, make that your routine. If you enjoy listening to 30 minutes of your audiobook, synchronize that with a walk around the neighborhood. Find what works for you and be willing to adjust it as necessary.

Chapter 4 – Reduce distractions...
Physically

I am saying this for your benefit, not to place restrictions on you. I want you to do whatever will help you serve the Lord best, with as few distractions as possible.
- 1 Corinthians 7:35

risis mode. I had become addicted to the convenience of fast food – and it was evidenced by my waistline and my lethargy. I was eating fast food at least 3 to 4 times each week for dinner. This was in addition to eating lunch out five times a week! My kitchen had turned into a desolate wasteland, a relic of times past. There was always something in the refrigerator: a quart of milk, some ice cream, strawberry jam, butter, (some leftover food from eating out), and frozen waffles. The cupboards were also suffering from neglect. A surprise inspection would likely reveal a bag of chips, a loaf of bread, peanut butter, a box of cookies, and a collection of ketchup and barbecue sauce packets from various fast food restaurants. It would take a finalist from one of those cooking competition television shows to pull together any type of meal with this combination of ingredients.

Minimize empty calories by keeping healthy snacks available.

My addiction confession

I would like to present my argument as to why I suffered from an addiction to eating out. (Just recognize it is nothing more than an intelligently crafted excuse). I was working at an accounting firm where the culture was working 10+ hours each day. In fact, there is a time period between January and April called "busy season" when every client-facing professional is required to report a minimum of 50 billable hours each week. The idea was if you can finish your weekly assignment in 40 hours, then raise your hand and the firm would find another 10 hours of work for you. Some weeks during that January through April time period, they would require a minimum of 55 billable hours a week.

This may seem outrageous, but we actually worked 50-60 hours on a normal week. I would get to the office around 7:30am and would not leave until around 7:30pm. That is 12 hours, take away an hour or so for lunch that still leaves 10 or 11 hours each day. Unlike my colleagues, I was intentional about avoiding working on weekends but sometimes it was just necessary. That would easily be another 4 to 6 hours added to the work week.

Here is the rub. The firm had an "overtime meal" policy to reward us for our hard work. If an employee worked more than 10 billable hours in a day, he or she could purchase a meal up to $16 dollars. At the end of each pay period, the employee submits the meal receipts and the firm would reimburse them. Hence, the low inventory in my kitchen. I could not get reimbursed for receipts from a grocery store!

I would work 10 hours each day, and then on my way home stop off at a fast food restaurant to purchase dinner. $16 dollars goes a long way when you are sitting in a drive-thru, and yes I wanted to get as close to that limit as possible. Large size? Yes. Any dessert? Yes. Double the patty? Sure. Even when I was conscious enough to avoid restaurants with drive thru lines, $16 is still more than enough for one person. I'll have the 3 meat combo. I'll also take a side of creamy potato salad. I'll add a peach cobbler to the order. What I did not eat that evening, I could eat on the weekend or share with someone else in the house. I would take that meal home, turn on the television around 8:30pm and take on the challenge of seeing how much gluttony one could pull off while watching a one hour episode of the Sopranos or Oz. Then I would roll into the bedroom – full and satisfied. The convenience, the money savings, the taste, the smell – I was addicted to it all.

Time fatigue

I do not beat myself up too much because I was suffering from time fatigue. I simply did not have enough time in the day to think about what I was eating. I woke up early to start my day, worked my butt off all day, rushed to get home to participate in my son's youth sports activities or my daughter's after-school programs, obsessed over spending quality time with my extended family, and had enough money and resources to support alternative eating habits. It was a conscious decision to focus my attention in other places – and I was struggling physically for that decision.

When we do not get enough sleep, we make poor decisions. When we do not do the things that inspire us, we make poor decisions. Single parents experience this a lot. The single dad has to get the kids ready for school, get to work, field phone calls from the school about late homework, behavior, upcoming events, pick the kids up from school, help with homework, resolve the debates over who had which toy first, get the kids ready for bed, and start the next day. What did I miss?

Oh yes, breakfast, lunch and dinner. Aren't there already enough things to do - how about a sausage burrito or donut holes for breakfast? How about a few slices of pizza or chow mein for dinner? This is not a sad story, this is the reality of many single parents' lives. We ask them to be everything to their children, and when they slip in any one area we are so quick to criticize them for not doing their part to raise responsible citizens in our society.

Things are much different now, compared to when I was working in the accounting firms. There are food delivery services, some who will send you prepackaged healthy meals that only require you to heat and serve. Nevertheless, that still takes time and it takes money – more money that it would cost to purchase the ingredients yourself from a grocery store and prepare the meal. So what has not changed is we are still asking people to choose between spending money and convenience or saving money and spending time. Many people, particularly single parents, do not have the luxury of making those decisions.

Turning the corner

Eventually I put my foot down and said "I will only eat one burger each week". I am embarrassed to admit how difficult that was for me. I did not change my eating-out habits, I just changed what I was ordering. It seemed like the more I wanted to avoid the burger, the more I craved it. It took me about a year of failure before I abandoned that strategy. I was left feeling worthless because I was unable to accomplish such a relatively simple task.

Years later, I converted to "Meatless Monday" and "Water Wednesday". On Mondays, I would not eat any meat. On Wednesdays, I would only eat seafood and no meat. When I undertook this novel approach, I was starting to get my eating habits back on track but I found this also to be untenable. I found myself just not eating on Mondays. It was like my body was protesting like a 6 year old, "If I can't eat what I want then I will eat nothing" and then my mind would respond "Okay, if that is what you want then fine – eat nothing". (Yes, that is how I talk to myself.). I even had the support of my wife – she was cooking vegetarian meals on Mondays and meals with seafood on Wednesdays. I could not sustain it though. I could not mentally accept what I 'could not' eat.

What eventually turned the corner for me was moving away from big meals to small meals. I became intentional about grazing: mindfully eating throughout the day. This prevented me from getting to the point in the day when I was just hungry (another time that leads to poor decisions).

People who eat frequent, small meals, as compared to people who gorge on a few big meals a day, suffer less colon cancer, have steadier moods, are less likely to develop diabetes, tend to be leaner, have less illnesses that end in "-itis" (arthritis, colitis, dermatitis, colitis). Small meal eaters also have a healthier immune system, enjoy lower levels of stress hormones, lower blood cholesterol, and generally just live longer and healthier. When we graze our body has less metabolic messes to get entangled in. By eating smaller amounts of food more frequently, we have less indigestion, heartburn, and other undesirables flowing through our blood vessels. Also, our insulin levels remain stable, which also leads to more stable weight.

Comparatively, a gorger who eats a high-fat, $16 meal leads to artery-damaging fats that clog the bloodstreams, cling to the lining of the arteries, contribute to plaque and the ultimately risk of stiffening the arteries. My body (your body, our bodies) is not designed to waste food, so it also pours out the food-storage hormone, insulin, to deposit excess food fats into my body's storage bank – belly fat! The three rules of grazing are:

1. Eat twice as often.
2. Eat half as much.
3. Chew twice as long.

My car, my rules

I have two rules when you ride in my car: 1) No farting and 2) No eating. I really appreciate a clean car; looks good, smells good. Eating in the car leaves crumbs on the seat, bags on the floor, and the residual smell of whatever has been enjoyed. (And farting, well that is self explanatory). I have to share these car rules because in order to turn the corner on my eating habits I had to modify one of those rules. I now keep a can of snack nuts or trail mix under the seat in my car. When I am driving home from work or on a long trip, I can reach under the seat and grab a snack and start grazing.

Do you want to know when I find myself reaching for this can underneath my seat most often? When I pass a sign that is yellow and is sneakingly shaped like an 'M'. This is not a coincidence. The color of a fast food sign is tremendously important and some colors have been subliminally etched into our minds to represent certain things. Red and yellow colors have become synonymous with fast food and for many people when they think of the two colors, inevitably it is fast food that pops into their head. Karen Haller, an expert in color psychology, has researched and discussed the psychological effects that these two colors have on people. "The feelings, the mood this combination of colors emits is perfect for their target market", Haller said. "Looking at the positive psychology qualities of red and yellow in relation to the fast food industry, red triggers stimulation, appetite, hunger, it attracts attention. Yellow triggers the feelings of happiness and friendliness ... when you combine red and yellow it's about speed, quickness. In, eat and out again." Haller added, "Yellow is also the most visible color in the daylight, which is why the ... M can be seen from a far distance".

So as we are driving through our normal day, we are going to be inundated with distractions. Signs and symbols that tempt us to pick up a quick bite to eat. We all know these meals, while they smell so good – they lack taste and, especially, lack nutritional value.

If you look in my kitchen today, it is stocked with bananas, yogurt, and nuts; small snacks that are healthy and can quench my immediate hunger. Of course, there are still some leftover fast food meals. I have not given this up completely (yet). However, I have become much more conscious of when I eat out and why I am eating out. Plus, I no longer get my meals reimbursed!

Chapter 5 – Start small and gradually increase...Physically

He replied, "Because you have so little faith. Truly I tell you, if you have faith as small as a mustard seed, you will say to this mountain, 'Move from here to there' and it will move. Nothing will be impossible for you".
-Matthew 17:20

hewbacca Kashykk. My first and only puppy. May he rest in peace. He lived a tumultuous life and died a tragic death. Chewie was a boxer and I brought him home when he was 6 weeks old. I fell in love with him instantly. I can still hear his incessant cry in the middle of the night as he lay in the blue crate near my bed. I remember sleepless nights and eventually caving and picking up Chewie to sleep in the bed with me. I also vividly remember when Chewie figured out how to crawl out of the blue crate; he started wandering around the house in the middle of the night. I had to start sleeping with the bedroom door closed to keep him from exploring. Until I found a pile of dog waste on my carpet near the door of my master bedroom.

That is when I bought a metal crate, and placed it in the kitchen of my small house to keep to Chewie confined at night. That crate was his home (err, prison) at night. He would cry, fight, scratch and claw to avoid getting put in there every day. We had a love/hate relationship, but mostly love.

As Chewie became an adolescent, his muscles grew and his muzzle features became pronounced. He was a mean-looking dog, but really a playful kid (actually, I despise when other dog owners tell me that about their own dog who is leaping towards me). I started taking Chewie out for walks around the neighborhood, but my neighborhood at the time was not the safest – okay, my neighborhood at the time was not safe. I did not feel safe walking more than 2 blocks in either direction from my home. It was deep East Oakland and things happened.

Little goals will build your confidence. Make a goal of walking a mile, then walking two miles, then running two miles.

I began taking Chewie to Lake Merritt, a beautiful lake in downtown Oakland. Always vibrant with lots of action going on. You can always find walkers, runners, bicyclists, moms with strollers, dads with toddlers, and dog walkers. I started walking the 3 mile radius lake and always was impressed with the people who could run the entire lake. I decided I should give it a try.

I couldn't even run for 5 minutes or 1/3 mile. I'll blame it on Chewie. Chewie was so excited to be out and running that he dragged me, and I could not keep up. (The truth was I was out of shape – too much accounting and excel spreadsheets while eating in my chair). I started making small goals, I'll run for 5 minutes and walk for 10 minutes. I'll run for 7 minutes and walk for 7 minutes. I'll run for 10 minutes and walk for 5 minutes. Chewie did not like the stopping, but like I said, we had a love/hate relationship.

Easy does it.

I talk to a lot of people who have these lofty goals of losing 20 pounds before (fill in the blank: wedding, summer, vacation, school starts, etc.). I ask them why are you aiming to lose so much weight, and why not just aim to lose 5 pounds? Because 5 pounds is not enough obviously. I'll let you guess whether these people meet their goal of losing 20 pounds... You are right, they don't.

I am not suggesting losing 20 pounds is not a reasonable, worthwhile goal. Some people really do need to lose 20 pounds or more. It could be for cosmetic, superficial reasons and it can also be for legitimate health reasons. What I am suggesting is why lose 20 pounds and hit one goal when you can lose 5 pounds 4 times and hit four goals. It is like having a graduation ceremony at the end of our freshmen, sophomore, junior, and senior year of high school. Find the little things to celebrate.

Everybody loves to win! It is embedded in our society. Achieving a goal is a win and it should be celebrated. The problem is that we set our first goal too high – so when we lose 10 pounds we feel like a failure. Or at least we feel like we could have done more. So instead of celebrating two successes of losing 5 pounds (for a total of 10 pounds), we wallow in one big disappointment (of not losing 20 pounds).

You know yourself better than I or anybody else. You know if losing 5 pounds is really a goal or not. Today, running one mile is not an achievement for me. It is not a worthwhile goal to celebrate. Similarly, you do not want to set a goal that can be easily achieved – and does not allow you to stretch yourself. So maybe it is not 4 goals of losing 5 pounds, but instead it is 2 goals of losing 10 pounds. Whatever gets you to your ultimate goal is small steps.

The most iconic villain of all time

And the award for the greatest movie villain of all time goes to... Darth Vader, the towering, black-clad menace. His head is covered by a mechanical helmet and the sound of his breathing is an eerie, mechanical hiss. Once a heroic Jedi Knight named Anakin Skywalker, Darth Vader was seduced by the dark side of the Force, and became a Sith Lord who served at the behest of Emperor Palpatine to eradicate the Jedi Order, instill the Galatic Empire across the galaxy, and contribute to the loss of 2 billion innocent lives on the planet of Alderaan.

There are three reasons why many people choose Darth Vader as the greatest movie villain of all time.

One, he is mysterious. We do not get to see his face until the last few minutes of the third film (i.e., Episode VI) leaving us to wonder – who is this man (or machine) and why is he so evil? We are left wondering what evil really looks like.

Two, his voice is dark and deep. He speaks very few words - and his most iconic line is only five words: "No, I am your father." Even when he is not speaking, his presence is felt through the intimidating sounds of his breathing.

Three, his appearance and outfit. His tall and bold structure and his calm and clean composure provides a perfect harmony of fear and reverence. His black armor is so shiny you can see your own terrified face. His blinking chest plate with red and white buttons, serving as a constant warning sign. His long flowing black cape opens just enough to see his most prized weapon, a lightsaber, hanging at his side ready to slice off the hand of anyone who stands in his way (including his own son).

I did not need to give that much detail for you to visualize Darth Vader. Whether or not you watch Star Wars religiously, you can recognize Darth Vader.

Darth Vader first appeared in "Episode IV, A New Hope" which was released in 1977. In that entire movie which lasted 121 minutes, Darth Vader appeared for only 9 minutes and 15 seconds. That is only 7.4% of the movie. George Lucas started small. In 1981, "Episode V, The Empire Strikes Back" was released. This movie was 124 minutes, and Darth Vader appeared for only 13 minutes and 15 seconds. That equates to 10.5% of the movie. George Lucas gradually increased it. In 1983, "The Return of the Jedi, Episode VI" was released. This movie lasted 131 minutes and featured Darth Vader in 14 minutes and 45 seconds of the film. This is 10.7% of the movie. George Lucas gradually increased it again. (There is "Episode III, Revenge of the Sith", released in 2005 when Darth Vader appears to say "Noooooooo!!!", but let's not go there). So in 376 minutes of film time, the most iconic villain had only 37 minutes and 15 seconds. Starting small can lead to a huge impact.

Monday afternoons

I wanted to encourage my mom and sister to get active. So I came up with a plan – let's meet on Monday afternoons at 4pm at the marina in San Leandro and we can walk and talk. This was a spin on an idea I had a few years before when my friends and I would meet at the marina golf course at 4pm for a round of 9 holes of golf. It was a great way to get out of the office and enjoy the long summer days, while fellowshipping with friends.

My mom and sister were initially hesitant. By this time, I was officially a runner. I could bang out 3 miles in less than 30 minutes with no preparation needed. I enjoyed running for 6-10 miles over the weekend. I had to reassure them I was not planning to run, I just wanted to walk with them. We also had to agree to the distance. My opening negotiation was 2 miles, and their collective response was "never mind". That is not how negotiations are supposed to work. I brought them back to the negotiation table and offered one mile. They agreed and the plan was set. I figured it would take about one hour to walk a mile with them, so I prepared for a slow walk with some great conversation.

The first Monday afternoon, we met near the park at the marina and took off towards the walking path hugging the San Francisco Bay. I set my watch for 30 minutes so I knew when we had to turn around. In my mind, I figured we would end up walking two miles anyways because we were having such great conversation and it was such a nice day. When my timer went off at 30 minutes I looked at the distance we had covered – less than 1/2 a mile. I did not mention it though. We turned around and returned back to our cars. It was a success. We had one hour of exercise, laughs, idea sharing, sweat, and love. We agreed to meet again next week, same place, same time.

The following Monday afternoon, we walked for one hour and slightly more than 1 mile. We were enjoying each other's company and the exercise. My mom got excited and bought new tennis shoes in preparation for our new weekly routine. We continued this routine for most of the summer. At the end, we were walking close to

2 miles and slightly more than one hour. We celebrated the effort, not the outcome - and still were able to achieve results.

If she can do it, so can I

I am a competitor. I will compete in anything: hopscotch, tether ball, basketball, frisbee throwing, dominoes, spelling bees, you name it. I just love the thrill of competition – and I love winning.

Eventually Chewie and I were able to increase our distance running around the lake, but I still was not able to make it the entire 3 miles. I concluded that it was not possible. The lake is a circle – so you park your car and head right towards the Alameda County courthouse. You keep walking around until you are back at your car. So obviously, I would see people running by me but I didn't know how long they ran because I would not see them again. I reasoned in my mind that everyone was doing what I was doing. Running for a while, then walking. I just happened to see them during the running portion of their exercise. In actuality, it was just another excuse I was telling myself because I could not run all three miles.

One day as I was walking during the 'walking portion' of my exercise with Chewie I ran into a friend who was out in her workout gear. She was... healthy. She was not the fittest person – I'm struggling to say it but... she did not look like the person who would run the lake. As we were talking she mentioned that she was about to "run the lake". I responded – "the whole lake?". She laughed, "yeah". Then she told me that her goal was to actually run the lake two times and she was working towards that goal. Maybe my facial expression gave it away – I hope it did not. I was floored that she was able to run the lake, and equally shocked that I was not able to.

A few days later, I found myself at the lake with a new resolve. Chewie and I were going to run the entire lake. I bent down and stared Chewie in the face and told him our goal. He didn't understand, but he sure appreciated that we did not have to stop. I did it – and have been doing it every since.

Sometimes, the biggest hurdle to achieving our goals is not external, but internal. We tell ourselves that we cannot do something and therefore we don't even make it a goal. We are giving ourselves an out, before we even step in. I did not start with the goal of running the entire 3 mile lake. I started slowly and met the first goal, then the next goal, and then the next goal. Many years later while training for a half marathon, I ran the lake 3 times. A total of 9 miles, stopping at my car each time to drink my sports drink and replenish my energy chews. Again, a goal I would not have imagined when I could not run five minutes consecutively.

Make a goal to walk around the block every night before or after dinner. Once you achieve that goal, make it a two- or three-block walk. You will find, with consistency, that the 3-block stretch goal you set was laughable when you are now walking the entire neighborhood. Headband and wristbands optional.

Chapter 6 – Educate yourself...
Physically

If any of you lacks wisdom, you should ask God, who gives generously to all without finding fault, and it will be given to you.
-James 1:5

R emember the Atkins diet? It is a diet devised by cardiologist Robert Atkins in the 1960s, and is considered one of the most popular low-carb, high-protein fad diets on the market, with claims of helping people lose up to 15 pounds in the first two weeks on the diet. The Atkins diet does work. It works by limiting a dieter's carbohydrate intake and increasing fiber intake, so the body burns fat instead of carbohydrates. It includes four phases; the first phase has dieters limit carbohydrate intake but encourages guilt-free consumption of protein-rich meat and fish, eggs, cheese, salad vegetables, butter and oil. With each subsequent phase, dieters add in more carbohydrates until they find the balance where they are no longer gaining weight from their diet. Sounds promising, so does friends helping friends.

Know how many calories you need to burn each day. Set targets around those benchmarks.

Friends helping friends

When I was a few years out of college I heard about a "can't lose" investment strategy, called Friends helping

Friends. I personally knew several friends who made $400, $800, $1,200 in a matter of days. If that is what they could achieve in days, imagine what can be amassed in months?! The investment worked because one friend (Buddy A) would recruit two friends (Buddy B). Each friend would contribute $50 to the fund. (The fund now has $100 and 3 "friends"). Those two friends (Buddy B) would then each recruit two friends (Buddy C) who would each contribute $50 to the fund. (The fund now has $300 and 7 "friends"). Each of those four friends (Buddy C) would then contribute $50. Each of those four friends (Buddy C) would then each recruit two friends (Buddy D) who would each contribute $50 to the fund. (The fund now has $700 and 15 "friends").

At this point, the first friend would now withdraw $400 from the fund and split the fund in two. (Each remaining fund now has $300 and 7 "friends"). After the fund splits into two – Buddy B becomes Buddy A, Buddy C becomes Buddy B, Buddy D becomes Buddy C and Buddy C each recruit two more friends. For those who get in early, they can turn $50 into $400, an 800% increase in a matter of days. (Except the first person who started the fund, she ends up with $400 with zero investment).

When I was first approached with this investment strategy I passed. It seemed too good to be true, and let's be honest – I did not have $50 to invest. As each day passed, I heard from the same friends and different friends (who ran in the same circle), telling me how they now have their own fund and are expecting $400 in the next day or so. I would also hear from friends who had just cashed out their own fund. I also saw the evidence of the $400 – a new jacket or a free lunch on them. Each day, with each story I was getting more and more antsy, I didn't want to miss out.

Eventually I took the plunge, I gave someone $50 in an envelope. The envelope was damp because of all the sweat on my palms. I waited and waited. The next day I asked for an update, and I had moved up. I didn't even have to recruit someone, the head of the fund was doing the recruiting for me! I waited and waited. The next day I asked for an update, voicemail. Well, I reasoned, no time to answer calls when you are busy making 800% return on investments. I waited and waited. The next day I asked for an update, voicemail. The next day, voicemail full. A couple decades later... I am still waiting for my $50 back – while also accepting the reality I fell for a pyramid scheme.

It may seem far-fetched to compare a pyramid scheme to fad diets but they work similarly. A pyramid scheme has tremendous upside in the beginning, but eventually it peters out and then has negative impacts.

Deconstructing the Atkins diet

The Atkins diet claims you can lose 15 pounds in the first two weeks of phase 1 – but it also acknowledges that those aren't typical results. The Atkins diet also acknowledges that you may initially lose water weight. It says that you'll continue to lose weight in phases 2 and 3 as long as you do not eat more carbohydrates than your body can tolerate. Most people can lose weight on almost any diet plan that restricts calories – at least in the short term. Over the long term, though, studies show that low-carb diets are no more effective for weight loss than are standard weight-loss diets.

Most people regain the weight they lost regardless of the diet plan. Because carbohydrates usually provide over half of calories consumed, the main reason for weight loss on the Atkins diet is lower overall calorie intake from eating less carbs. Other reasons for weight loss is because your food choice is limited, and you eat less since the extra protein and fat keep you feeling full longer. Both of these effects also contribute to lower overall calorie intake.

The Atkins diet professes that its eating plan can prevent or improve serious health conditions, such as metabolic syndrome, diabetes, high blood pressure and cardiovascular disease. In fact, nearly any diet that helps you shed excess weight reduces risk factors for cardiovascular disease and diabetes. Further, most weight-loss diets improve blood cholesterol or blood sugar levels, at least temporarily. There are no major studies to show whether these benefits hold up for the long term or increase how long you live. Conversely, some health experts believe that eating a large amount of fat and protein from animal sources can increase your risk of heart disease, however it is not known what risks, if any, pose over long term.

This is not an indictment on the Atkins diet. This is a plea to educate yourself and know what you are getting yourself into. Before jumping into the next viral sensation, conduct your own research and decide whether this plan works for what you are seeking to accomplish. If you need to lose 15 pounds in the next two weeks and are fine gaining it back two months later – then visit the nearest Brazilian Steakhouse and enjoy yourself.

Less calories each day = less weight

The formula is simple – if you want to lose weight, you need to move more and eat less. The truth is we need to eat every day, and we need to sit/sleep every day. So to make this simple formula even more basic – To lose 1 or 2 pounds per week, you will need to burn 500 to 1,000 calories more than you eat each day – or 3,500 to 7,000 calories each week.

The total number of calories you burn in a day depends on things like your age, height and weight, muscle mass and how much you exercise. There are several formulas to calculate your exact total daily energy expenditure or TDEE. A detailed look at your TDEE requires four factors:

1. Resting Metabolic Rate (RMR) – this is the total number of calories your body needs each day for basic functions. Using the Harris-Benedict equation: A man's RMR = 88.362 + (29.473 x weight in pounds) + (12.167 x height in inches) - 5.677 x age in years). A woman's RMR = 447.593 + (20.343 x weight in pounds) + (7.869 x height in inches) - 4.330 x age in years).

2. Thermic Effect of Food (TEF) – the calories your body uses to digest, absorb and store the nutrients from the food you eat. Certain foods have a higher thermic effect than others – such as foods high in protein and fiber.

3. Nonexercise Activity Thermogenesis (NEAT) – this is the number of calories your body uses doing daily activities, like brushing your teeth, washing dishes and walking. This number varies greatly from person to person, and day to day depending on your level of activity.

4. Calories burned during exercise – this calculates the number of calories you burn during a workout.

The number depends on how long and how intensely you work out.

To calculate your TDEE, you take your RMR and multiply by your activity level. A sedentary life gets a 1.2 factor; a lightly active life gets a 1.375 factor; a moderately active life gets a 1.55 factor; a very active life gets a 1.725 factor; and an extra active life gets a 1.9 factor.

To lose weight, you first calculate your TDEE to get your maintenance calories. Then subtract that number by 500-1,000. You achieve this calorie deficit by eating fewer calories, burning more calories through NEAT and exercise or a combination of the two.

Is your head spinning? Well, it should be spinning a bit. This is all a part of educating yourself. Our realm of knowing things can be separated into three broad categories: what we know, what we know we don't know and what we don't know we don't know. Allowing your mind to be stretched, by moving knowledge from 'what you don't know you don't know' to 'what you know you don't know'. It does not need to be this complicated, but it can be even more complicated – or more simple.

What is most important is that you decide what your target is, based on some legitimate research, and then aim to complete that goal. Do not settle for the first-come, first-served mentality. Set a target that is achievable in the long run because being healthy is not a destination, it is a life journey.

It's much more than pounds

Watching your weight is one way to measure your body's health, but there are other ways as well. This is all a part of being proactive and researching the information you need to fit your lifestyle and goals. Below are some other common ways to measure health and fitness:

- Body Mass Index or BMI is calculated based on your height and weight. The calculation helps your doctor tell if you may be at risk for health problems because of your weight. One disadvantage of this method is that it does not provide any information about body fat. It also tends to be less accurate for people who are very muscular or very short.
- Waist circumference is a simple test you can conduct right now. Measure around your waist at the level of the belly button in inches. If you are a man with a measurement higher than 40 or a women with a measurement higher than 35, then you are at increased risk for certain health problems like heart disease and stroke. Again, this approach does not give insight into your body composition or fat percentage.
- Skinfold calipers measures body fat. It is a measuring device that pinches the skin and tissues at certain places on the body to estimate body fat. No matter what you weigh, the higher percentage of body fat you have, the more likely you are to develop obesity-related diseases, including heart disease, high blood pressure, stroke, and type 2 diabetes.
- Body fat scales are available for use at home. These scales work by sending seemingly-harmless electrical current through the body to detect fat and lean tissue, providing a reading of your body-fat percentage. The devices vary in accuracy, but they can be good for tracking changes over time.
- Dual-energy X-ray absorptiometry, or DEXA is a test that measures bone density by sending two X-ray beams at different peak energy frequencies to the

target bones. One peak is absorbed by soft tissue and the other by bone. It specifically identifies fat deposits and determines body-fat percentage. These emerging-technology scanning machines are typically offered by medical offices.

These are very general statements. It is extremely important you learn about your own body and the foods that you put into your own body. The more you know about your body, the better you can take care of it. And the more you know, the more equipped you will be at detecting any changes that you should discuss with your doctor or health care provider.

I concluded many years ago to keep the ball in my court. I do not expect others to always keep my best interests at heart, so I learned how to conduct my own research and build my own knowledge. I freely share this knowledge, when asked.

PART II

LIVING
SPIRITUALL
Y
HEALTHY

Chapter 7 – Do it first...Spiritually

I rise before dawn and cry for help; I have put my hope in your word.
-Psalms 119:147

The alarm went off at 5:40am on Wednesday morning. This gave me 10 minutes to visit the toilet, wash my face and throw on a matching sweatsuit. I had to be out the door by 5:50am in order to make the 10 minute drive to my church. My pastor had asked on Sunday morning, "who is going to join me at 6am for prayer on Wednesday? Stand up." I stood up. Partially because I succumbed to the pressure of others standing around me; partially because I needed some extra prayer time to repair my broken life.

The 6:00am prayer service always started the same. Someone read Ephesians 6:10 – *"Finally be strong in the Lord and the power of his might. Put on the whole armor of God, so that you can stand against the devil's schemes. For our struggle is not against flesh and blood, but against rulers, against the authorities, against the powers of this dark world and against spiritual forces of evil in the heavenly realms. Therefore, put on the whole armor of God, so that when the day of evil comes, you may be able to stand your ground, and after you have done everything, to stand. Stand firm then, with the belt of truth buckled around your waist, with the breastplate of righteousness in place, and with your feet fitted with the readiness that comes from the gospel of peace. In addition to all of this, take up the shield of faith, with which you can extinguish all the flaming arrows of the evil one. Take the helmet of salvation and the sword of the Spirit, which is the word of God."* This was followed by several other familiar scriptures. We always ended the opening scriptures with 1 Timothy 2:8 *"Therefore I want the men everywhere to pray, lifting up holy hands without wrath or doubting."* Then we would sing some worship songs, before kneeling down for individual prayer. Then we would rise again for corporate prayer. At 7am, we would end the prayer service and start our day. Some would leave the church and head straight to work. I needed to go back home to prepare myself for work (matching sweatsuits were not suitable work attire for an accountant) – with a renewed mind and positive outlook on the day ahead.

Find 5-10 minutes in the morning to meditate on goodness and mercy and strength

Opening scenes

I am a connoisseur of Star Wars. Each Star Wars movie begins with something exciting happening. In Episode 4, the Rebel Alliance is running away from Darth Vader after just receiving the blueprints detailing the flaws in the Death Star. In Episode 1, two Jedis arrive for peaceful negotiations for a trade dispute with the Viceroy only to find themselves in an unexpected battle with droids. George Lucas, a master of storytelling, knows that the start of the movie sets the stage for the rest of the movie. You want to capture the audience and set expectations for what is to come. Similarly, we should be the director of the movie that plays in our mind each day.

Each morning we have the opportunity to set the stage for the rest of the day. I used to start each day by watching the morning news (until I realized that the news cycle became more about entertainment and propaganda) and it unintentionally set the compass of my day filled with fear about budget cuts, anxiety about stock market declines, frustrations about unavoidable traffic jams, disappointment by the anticipated rain in the afternoon. Instead of letting a news cycle (whether it be the television or FaceBook or Twitter) be your opening scene, why not make a conscious choice on what you will allow to start your day. You can choose faith over fear, peace over anxiety, acceptance over frustration, and appreciation over disappointment.

This is not a natural occurrence. If left to fate, you will find things to take you off your path of faith, peace, acceptance, and appreciation. You have to be intentional.

Imperfect prayers work too

The early 90s were transition years for me. I was coming into my own after watching one brother graduate from high school and embark upon college and watching another brother embark upon a career as a street hustler and pimp. I was still experimenting with different crowds and scenes, personalities and music. Okay, I admit it...I was an MC Hammer fan. Yes, I wore the baggy pants and the polka dot shirts. I bought the knock-off Gazelle glasses and popped the lenses out the frame. I rocked a high-top fade and could mimic every dance move from MC Hammer to Kid 'n Play to Heavy D and the Boyz. I did have my limits though – I never was a fan of Vanilla Ice or Marky Mark and the Funky Bunch.

Mark Wahlberg is quite the character - and he is evidence that you do not need to be perfect to pray. He first popped on the celebrity scene as Marky Mark and the

Funky Bunch in the early 1990s. He was riding on the fame of his older brother, Donnie Wahlberg from New Kids on the Block. In 2010, Wahlberg told the Catholic Herald that his religion was "the most important aspect of my life." He prays daily, saying "The first thing I do when I start my day is, I get down on my hands and knees and give thanks to God...If I can start my day out by saying prayers and getting myself focused, then I know I'm doing the right thing. That 10 minutes helps me in every way throughout the day."

Mark Wahlberg has grown from his 'rapping' days, and is now a very successful actor and producer. My favorite work of art from his is executive producer credits on the show, "Entourage". I also enjoyed him in films like "Four Brothers" and "The Departed". He is undoubtedly talented.

It is amazing how God can orchestrate events in your life. Wahlberg was booked to fly on American Airlines Flight 11 on September 11, 2001, but his plans changed the day before and he canceled his reservation. But even in God's perfected plan, we find ways to screw things up. In a 2012 interview, he stated "If I was on that plane with my kids, it wouldn't have went down like it did". Yeah, he didn't need to say that. Also, Mark had some racially-charged incidents during his teenage years which led to civil and criminal penalties. Years later, he attempted to get pardoned for these crimes (which did not happen).

Nevertheless, despite his successes, and his imperfections, he manages to make prayer a part of his morning ritual. He recognizes that how he starts his day affects the rest of his day.

Read, Write, Recite

I have found three methods to focus on goodness, mercy and strength each morning. Each one of them has different benefits and serves different purposes.

The first morning method is reading. Rewind a few decades, my church would always have fresh pocket-sized books of Daily Bread delivered each quarter. It would be three months of daily meditations and scriptures that take anywhere from 1-4 minutes to read. Today, those pocket-size books are hard to find but I keep the Daily Bread app on my smartphone. And sometimes I choose to start the day with reading the daily inspiration. I also have a Bible app on my phone and participate in 3-day or 7-day bible plans that give me a theme to follow. There are benefits to reading in the morning. It improves our brain connectivity. Imagine your brain as a dirt path on a hiking trail, the more someone walks on that pathway it creates grooves in the ground that eventually look like a designed path. The more we read about God's goodness and grace and mercy, the more it settles into our brain, into our thoughts and into our actions.

A second morning method is writing. I keep a small notebook near my bed. Some days before I get out of bed, I force myself to think about something to be grateful for and I write it down in this notebook. You could write a short story, a few words, or just one word. Anything helps because writing things down helps to clear your mind and clarify your priorities. These daily musings also can serve as a motivational tool later. I have often picked up the notebook after having a tough meeting or grappling with a missed opportunity. It takes me back to a time in the day when I was able to more clearly see the joys of life. Of course, you can always type your notes into your smartphone but you miss the benefits of handwritten notes. Some of the benefits include effective memory recall, sharpened critical thinking, and stronger conceptual understanding. I hope my students are paying attention to this paragraph – simply put, you retain information better when you handwrite your notes as compared to typing them into your laptop or onto your smartphone.

A third morning method is reciting. This is actually the first method, supersized. Instead of reading silently, I read out loud. Reading aloud facilitates narrative transport – a state characterized by absorption into a story's narrative flow. It creates an opportunity for you to forget your surroundings and engage with the visual, auditory, kinesthetic and emotional senses - a sense of time distortion.

Colin MacLeod, a psychologist at the University of Waterloo in Canada, has extensively researched the impact of reading aloud on memory. McLeod and his team showed that people consistently remember words and texts better if they read them aloud, rather than reading them silently. This memory-boosting effect of reading aloud is especially strong in children, but it works for older people too. "It's beneficial throughout the age range," he says. McLeod has named this phenomenon the "production effect". It means that producing written words (i.e., reading them aloud) improves our memory of them. Recall my example earlier about the dirt pathway on a hiking trail resembling a designed path. Imagine how faster that pathway would be created if more people walked over it.

Chapter 8 – Forgive yourself...
Spiritually

Therefore, there is now no condemnation for those who are in Christ Jesus.
- Romans 8:1

here are five covenants in the Holy Bible: the Noahic Covenant, the Abrahamic Covenant, the Mosaic Covenant, The Davidic Covenant, and the New Testament. The Noahic Covenant is found in Genesis-Chapter 9 and this is the covenant that God establishes with Noah to preserve humanity and provide for the restraint of human evil and violence. The Abrahamic Covenant is also found in Genesis, Chapters 12 and 15. This is the covenant central to the biblical story, where God promises Abraham a land, descendants, and blessings - blessings that would extend to all the people of the earth. The Mosaic Covenant is in Exodus-Chapters 19 and 24, where God establishes a covenant with former enslaved people at Mount Sinai. With it, God supplied the laws for His people to follow. It was not intended to be a means to salvation, but rather to distinguish God's people from other surrounding people. The Mosaic covenant was conditional. It defined blessings and curses based on behaviors of obedience and disobedience. The Davidic Covenant is in 2nd Samuel where God promises David that his descendants would reign on the throne. It was a continuation of the Abrahamic Covenant that established land, descendants and blessings, but through a Messiah.

The New Covenant is best described in Jeremiah 31:31-34 and Luke 22:14-23. This is the language first used in Jeremiah's promise of rescue and renewal of God's people. It promises a coming day when God would make a new covenant unlike the Mosaic one which was eventually broken. This coming day would bring forgiveness of sin, internal renewal of the heart, and intimate knowledge of God. On the night of Jesus's Last Supper, Jesus takes the cup and declares that His death would be the inauguration of this new covenant. If you were born in the last 2,000 years (give or take a few centuries) – you are under the new covenant.

Recognize that your sins of the past do not define your present or future.

The New Covenant

The New Covenant is the penultimate solution to humanity's rebellious nature. As humans, we are all born in sin and shaped in iniquities, so we are predicated to sinful nature. In Jeremiah 31:33, the prophet declares *"This is the covenant I will make with the house of Israel after that time... I will put my law in their minds and write it on their hearts. I will be their God and they will be my people."* This New Covenant comes through the death of Jesus Christ. In Luke 22:20 Jesus says *"This cup is the new covenant in My blood, which is poured out for you."* This means we can go directly to God through Christ. There is forgiveness of sins only through the new covenant.

Under the Mosaic covenant, people had to atone for sins by offering sacrifices and other outside demonstrations for others to witness. Under the New covenant, our sins are forgiven through Christ's redemptive power. We no longer rely on what is on the outside, we focus inward – what is written in our hearts and monopolizing our minds.

It is a blessing to know that God forgives us for our sins (and our repeated sins). But can we forgive ourselves? Too often, we allow our sins to haunt us and they keep us from walking in confidence.

I said I was sorry

I was relaxing on the couch when I heard a bump, followed by silence, followed by a wail, followed by the footsteps of my wife running down the hall. I admiringly did not leave my comfortable position, but I listened intently as my older toddler son explained how he had hit my younger toddler son. As the younger toddler continued wailing louder and louder (clearly a ploy to get my wife's attention and sympathy), my older toddler sped up his words and raised his voice to explain himself. He eventually started crying also, and stated emphatically, "I said I was sorry".

After the commotion died down a bit, I walked into the other room and explained to my older toddler son that just because you are sorry does not excuse the behavior. His action, hitting his little brother, still hurt and there was going to be a reaction to his action.

My son expected forgiveness since he was apologetic, moreover, my son expected there to be no impeding response (no crying, no punishment) because he "said sorry". My son was only 5 years old at the time. I can understand his logic. For those of you reading this book, you have two, three, four plus decades on my son – but yet, we still carry this same childish logic. We can ask for forgiveness, but unless we pause and examine the reason for that behavior (or continuous behavior), are we really asking for forgiveness?

Forgive, but don't forget

There are a few things more foolish than refusing to learn lessons from the failings of those who have gone before us. Belshazzar, was the son and crown prince of Nabonidus, and the last king of the Babylonian Empire. He is believed to be the grandson of King Nebuchadnezzar.

King Nebuchadnezzar was a great ruler. He was blessed with riches, power and was very much respected in Babylon and surrounding empires. Unfortunately, the King took the gifts of his life for granted and he allowed pride to rule his life. He failed to acknowledge God as the one who provided him with the riches and power and eventually fell from grace. Pride eventually got into Nebuchadnezzar's head when he said "is not this great Babylon, that I have built for the house of the kingdom by the might of my power, and for the honor of my majesty". This marked the beginning of his fall.

A voice from heaven fell down saying "O king, to thee it is spoken, the kingdom is departed from thee. And they shall drive thee from men, and thy dwelling shall be with the beasts of the field: they shall make thee to eat grass as oxen, and seven times shall pass over thee, until thou know that the most High ruleth in the kingdom of men, and giveth it to whomsoever he will".

Imagine the humility and ridicule the King endured as he was subjected to eat grass, could not shelter himself from inclement weather, and could not even afford a haircut! The King had lost his mind, and was living like a wild animal. Eventually, God granted King Nebuchadnezzar unmerited favor and restored him to the kingdom, and even added to his majestic rule.

Now you would think that if your grandfather lived through that experience, then you would be careful to not repeat his mistakes. However, Belshazzar was also filled with pride and made the same error of refusing to honor God, but instead celebrated his own power. Instead of applying the lessons of Nebuchadnezzar's fall, he chose to walk down the same path.

While it is important that we forgive ourselves for failures, it is also important that we do not allow ourselves to repeat those same mistakes. Forgiveness without a functional change will be futile.

The four Rs

Self-forgiveness is not about letting yourself off the hook nor is it a sign of weakness. The act of forgiveness, whether you are forgiving yourself (or someone who has wronged you), does not suggest that you condone the behavior. Forgiveness means that you:
- accept the behavior,
- you accept was has happened, and

69

- you are willing to move past it and move on with your life without ruminating over past events that cannot be changed.

Here are four steps to self-forgiveness: Responsibility, Remorse, Restoration, Renewal.

First, accept responsibility: face what you have done or what has happened and show compassion to yourself. For me, it is easier to show compassion to someone else than to myself. That is why I consider this the hardest step. I have to stop making excuses, rationalizing, or justifying my actions to make them seem okay – I just have to face up and accept what I did. Once I acknowledge that I engaged in actions that hurt my relationship with God and my relationship with others then I can avoid negative emotions, like excessive regret and guilt.

Second, embrace remorse. It is completely normal, even healthy, to feel guilty about something you have done wrong. These feelings of guilt are the launching pad to bringing positive behavior change. Very important: Focus on the guilt, less on the shame. Guilt implies you are a good person who did something bad. Shame suggests you are a bad person and unworthy of social interaction. Shame brings feelings of worthlessness, which can lead to addiction, depression, and aggression.

Third, restore the trust. It is important to make amends to have true forgiveness. The Bible says, all have sinned and fallen short of God's Glory. The Bible also says, that if we confess our sins God is faithful and just to forgive us and cleanse us from unrighteousness. Did Jesus suffer on the cross for nothing? We have an unopened gift box waiting for us each day, and that is the gift of forgiveness and redemption. We need to open that gift box every day and be thankful for its contents. When our sins impact others, we need to take action to rectify our mistakes. It may be as simple as a sincere apology, however, it may require an offer of compensation through our time or resources. Fixing our mistakes means we do not have to wonder if we could have done more.

Fourth, seek renewal. Avoid the temptation to fall into the trap of agonizing in self-hatred or pity. This can be damaging to our self-esteem and our motivation. When we forgive ourselves, we have to find a way to learn from the experience and grow as a person. This starts with us taking an honest look at why we behaved this way and what steps we can take to prevent this from happening again in the future. This process helps us make better choices in the future.

Remember, God's mercies are new every morning. The Hebrew word for "new" as used here is *chadash* meaning "fresh, new thing, to rebuild". The Hebrew word for "morning" as used here is *bouquer* meaning "dawn, to pour out, to spread out as a fruitful vine". Please pause to soak this illustration in your heart and mind. Every day, God promises us a rebuilding that will pour out and spread across all the lives we touch. All we have to do is ask for His refreshing. We should offer that same grace to ourselves, so we can receive His renewed strength.

Chapter 9 – Be consistent...
Spiritually

*"Let perseverance finish its work so that you may be mature and
complete, not lacking anything"*
- James 1:4

f there was an award show for Husband of the Year, I
would have won it in 2019. I imagine it would be the
last presentation of the awards gala, preceded by Best
Uncle, Best Stepfather of the Year, Best New Boyfriend of
the Year, Best Brother-in-Law, and Best Father-in-Law.
There would have been speeches and performances from
iconic television husbands Phil Dunphy, Andre Johnson,
Jack Pearson, and Randall Pearson. There would have
been performances by John Legend, Michael Buble and
Jay Z. "And the winner for best husband solely based on
his Christmas Gift for 2019 is..."

I would start my acceptance speech by thanking my
wife, because I am guessing in this fantasy award show I
would have needed her nomination or recommendation.
I would then thank Jeff Olson, the author of the book "The
Slight Edge: Turning Simple Disciplines into Massive
Success and Happiness" for the inspiration. In June of
2019, I read Jeff's book and was compelled to start
working on a Christmas gift for my wife. For the next 180
days I took 5 minutes each day to write down what I was
grateful for that day as it related to my wife. I wrote about
our lunch that day, our walk around the neighborhood,
our disagreement, our laughs over a movie, whatever
came to my mind as I reflected on that day. It took me no

more than 7 minutes each day. I know because I literally sat down with a 5 minute timer and just started writing until the timer ended. Once I heard the bell, I would finish the last thought and conclude.

What was less than 0.5% of my day's effort turned into an amazing, thoughtful gift that my wife has read over multiple times. It has led to some serious conversations, reliving good memories and learning from less favorable experiences. All because I was consistent.

Be consistent with your worship, your prayer, and your study. Create a reasonable and achievable plan.

Do you really?

I am always amazed when I talk with other believers who tell me they do not read the Bible, do not pray continuously, and do not give of their time and resources to the ministry. I won't say this to their face, but I am surely thinking "I wouldn't want to be friends with you". What type of true friendship does not involve some intimate time on a daily basis, or at least in regular intervals? And in those moments when true friends cannot be in contact with each other, there is a longing in my heart – something missing that I need my true friend to help fill. The response I hear from believers who are not being consistent is: "I want to do more...but I just don't have time." I tried that excuse before.

My firm was preparing me for leadership and introduced me to a life coach to help become a more well-rounded business professional. I was excited, but apprehensive to meet with the life coach. During our first official meeting she was asking me questions and immediately I felt comfortable enough sharing with her my real thoughts and concerns. The conversation lead me to musing about how much I work and how I did not have time for the things I really enjoy and want to do.

I offered her a "perfect example" of my music ministry. All throughout college and even in my first few years at the accounting firm, I was committed to singing in the choir. I would show up for choir practice on Thursdays at 7:30pm (sometimes even show up at 6:30pm for the praise and worship rehearsal) and I would sing on Sundays at the 8am and 11am worship service. It was something I enjoyed, and I also enjoyed the people I fellowshipped with in the choir. We were family.

I told the life coach, "I just don't have the time to do that anymore" and blinked my puppy dog eyes in her direction. I was hoping for some sympathy or perhaps some magic schedule fixer, instead she told me something that sticks with me to this day (and that I have re-shared verbally to anyone I counsel). She said "It's not that you don't have time, it's that you don't really want to do it". I immediately corrected her with a smug attitude, "Oh, that's not true. I really want to sing in the choir. I enjoy it and it is important to me." She calmly interrupted me, "We make time for the things that are important to us. Clearly, singing in the choir is not as important to you in this season of your life. If it was important, you would make time for it. You would move other things out of your schedule to make time."

I was left speechless. I did not end up working with this life coach, and as I reflect on that decision today I honestly think it was because I was not ready at the time for someone to read me so directly. She was absolutely right, and I have never rejoined the choir on a consistent basis.

Fervent and frequent

The Bible tells us about one of Paul's disciples, Epaphras who founded the church at Colossae. Paul writes to the Colossians church in Colossians 4:12: *"Epaphras, who is one of you and a servant of Christ Jesus, sends greetings. He is always wrestling in prayer for you, that you may stand firm in all the will of God, mature and fully assured. I vouch for him that he is working hard for you and for those at Laodicea and Hierapolis."*
I focus on the words "always wrestling in prayer" - a sign of consistency. I mention Epaphras because he was consistent in his prayer for others. Imagine how he prayed for himself and his family to be protected, blessed, mature, and fully assured. Be consistent with your worship, your prayer, and your study. Create a reasonable and achievable plan.
Our prayers need to be fervent and frequent. 1 Thessalonians 5:16-18 tells us to *"rejoice always, pray without ceasing, give thanks in all circumstances; for this is the will of God in Christ Jesus for you"*. Over the years I have found myself praying without ceasing. Please do not conjure up the image of me on bended knees, sweating while in an executive board room. Instead, imagine me muttering under my breath "God be with me" as I take my seat in the board room. Or, envision me shaking the hand of a colleague while thinking "God Bless her to see me as an ally, not an adversary". Or, picture me reading a scripture on my smartphone while sitting in the lobby

waiting on an important meeting to start. These are examples of small things that can take up less than 0.5% of your allotted minutes for the day but can have a significant impact on your life.

Day and night

Joshua was probably a teenager when Moses delivered God's people from slavery and started towards the Promised Land. Joshua ended up becoming Moses' second in command. Most of the adults who left bondage wandered in the wilderness and did not see the Promised Land. However, when Moses transitioned and Joshua became the leader, Joshua led the armies that conquered Canaan and distributed its land to the 12 tribes. Joshua implored his people to "keep this book of law always on your lips; meditate on it day and night, so that you may be careful to do everything written in it. Then you will be prosperous and successful".

I teach accounting at both the lower division courses and master's courses. I would love it for any of my students to meditate on the concepts of accounting day and night. It would make them very careful in completing the homework assignments error free and passing the exams with flying colors. The one piece I cannot guarantee them though is that if they pass my class with an A, then they will be prosperous and successful. I would have to own a meaningful share of the partnership in all 138,000 accounting firms to make that bold statement.

Yet here we see the word of God making us this promise that when we study His word diligently, both day and night and making it part of our everyday talk – then He will promise us prosperity and success. Do we believe Him? Do we believe God? Do we believe God's word? If so, this sounds like a no-brainer – sign me up.

It does not take a large commitment to learning God's word, but it does take consistency. Many years ago I was sitting in a bible study and the teacher asked "How many of you have read the entire Bible?". Most hands in that room, including mine, stayed on our laps. That question stuck with me for about four or five years before I realized I need to read the Bible for myself. Actually, why not tell the whole story...I was working with a colleague from our New York office who told me about this book called "The Story: The Bible as one Continuing Story of God and His People" by Max Lucado. I figured that was palatable so I bought the book and read it, quite fascinated.

After reading that I was encouraged to read the entire Bible. I did not start at Genesis 1:1 though. I relied on an app to guide me through the Bible in one year. It required me to read for about 20 minutes each day for one year. (20 minutes is 1.4% of your day). If I missed a day, no worries, I could read for 40 minutes the next day (2.8% of my day) or read for 30 minutes for the next two days (about 2% of my day). These small investments paid off hugely. One year later, I had read the entire Bible. This is no different than reading a book. When I read "The Story" (which is way more interesting than the Bible itself in my opinion) I did not finish that book in one sitting. I read lots of books and no matter how intrigued I am with the plot, the characters, the arc – I eventually put the book down and pick it up again later. This is how we live our lives, small contributions lead to big differences.

Me and you

I am meeting more Christians who attend the same church, "The Church by the side of the Bed". Yes I am referring to internet church. I do not discount the power and anointing of those pastors and bishops who run international ministries. I subscribe and regularly listen to several of them to have my soul challenged and inspired. But that cannot be all.

When I am not able to make it to my own church on a Sunday, it does not sit right with me. It is like being away from my own bed, I can do it for a few days or maybe even a week or two - but my soul longs for that comfort and convenience from being around other believers. Sunday morning used to be reserved for church service. Now Sunday morning competes with the NBA playoffs, NFL games (on the West Coast), youth sports, fancy brunches, travel days for conferences, etc. It leaves me empty and it is not what God intended.

Nehemiah 8 describes Ezra assembling the people of God to hear his word:

"And all the people gathered as one man into the square before the Water Gate. And they told Ezra the scribe to bring the Book of the Law of Moses that the Lord had commanded Israel. So Ezra the priest brought the Law before the assembly, both men and women and all who could understand what they heard, on the first day of the seventh month. And he read from it facing the square before the Water Gate from early morning until midday, in the presence of the men and the women and those who could understand. And the ears of all the people were attentive to the Book of the Law...And Ezra blessed the Lord, the great God, and all the people

79

answered, 'Amen, Amen', lifting up their hands. And they bowed their heads and worshiped the Lord with their faces to the ground."

God's word is not meant to be eaten alone. Imagine if you made a seven course meal (I'm imagining the dinner table at the opening scene of the 1997 movie, Soul Food) and only one person showed up to eat it. It would be disrespectful, and it would be a waste of good food. Let's not waste good food by trying to eat alone. We want to taste the smothered chicken and then turn to a friend with a head nod and thumbs up. We want to scoop the gravy and then open our mouths at the same time in awe at the bursting combination of spices. This is also God's word. We want to high-five each other when we hear a confirming word from the preacher. We want to cry on each other's shoulders when we are convicted and led to a new level of freedom in Christ. This starts by committing something: Sunday morning service, Sunday evening service, Tuesday Bible Study, Wednesday prayer call, Friday Bible Study. Something small can make a huge difference in our spiritual life when we stay consistent and build on it.

The power of prayer

If there is one place to start building consistency, it would be with prayer. Prayer is giving our attention to God in a two-way spiritual relationship. It is a conversation with a desire and intent to strengthen your relationship. As your relationship grows, you will be inclined to read more from the Bible, to spend more time with believers, to give of your resources more freely.

To create consistency in prayer you should first identify a prayer closet. It does not need to be a closet, it can be a bedroom, balcony, or even a chair facing a window. Just find a place where you can be comfortable and designate it as your prayer closet. When I was in high school I had a friend whose parents were Hindu. I visited their home and was shocked to see that one room was designated as an office and a place for prayer. There was always a level of reverence that even I showed when I walked past that room.

Next, keep your Bible or a Bible app nearby. I challenge you to simply open the Bible and start reading. Ask God to speak to you as you read the scriptures. Let God guide you in what to read and how to interpret. Two Bible books I would recommend are Proverbs and Psalms. Proverbs was written by King Solomon and is an example of the biblical-wise literature and addresses questions of values, moral behavior, the meaning of human life and right conduct. Psalms was written mostly by King David and offers us ways to rejoice in prayer, to bow in worship, to exalt God for all he does and for all his blessing to us. One of my consistent tasks was to copy by hand the entire book of Proverbs and Psalms. I still have those notebooks, which are highlighted and referenced.

Third, listen to God. Remember that prayer is a conversation, and no effective conversation is one-way. Learn to be comfortable in silence. I have never heard God's voice booming like thunder from the hills. However, I have heard God's voice in a scripture of the day, in a word of encouragement from a friend, in a lyric in a song on the radio. God is everywhere and when we open ourselves to Him fully, He will reveal Himself to us in many ways.

Fourth, we have to make prayer a priority. Find a specific time of day when you will pray. It could be before you step away from your desk for lunch. It could be on your second bathroom visit of the day. It could be on your morning walk. I have found that once I carved out a specific time and committed, it did not take too long to see the benefits of being in constant communication with Christ. I started finding more and more opportunities to pray.

Fifth, find an accountability prayer partner. Someone who you can pray with on a weekly basis. If you are married or in a committed relationship, your spouse or partner is the obvious choice. You can also look to your church for weekly prayer services. You can also look online for neighborhood churches that regularly hold prayer services online or over the phone or internet.

Consistency is the key to success in anything, including strengthening your spiritual life. Consistency leads to habits. Habits form the actions we take every day. Action leads to success. As Anthony Robbins said, "It's not what we do once in a while that shapes our lives."

Chapter 10 – Reduce distractions...
Spiritually

"Watch and pray so that you will not fall into temptation. The spirit is willing, but the flesh is weak."
- Matthew 26:41

My church has been "my church" for my entire life. My mom often retells the story of how the first time she received the Holy Ghost was while visiting the church when she was pregnant with me. Shortly after I was born, she changed her church membership and I have never known anything else.

My church has always been youth-centric: living the words of Proverbs Chapter 22, Verse 6 to *"train up a child in the way of the Lord and when that child is older he or she will not depart from the way of the Lord."*

Fellowship with others who are supportive of your faith, and your beliefs.

Every Sunday we had "children's church" which was held in our chapel (the size of many storefront churches). We had to sit on the correct side (girls sat on the left and boys sat on the right) and in the correct row (the younger you were, the closer you had to sit to the front of the chapel). We would go through each row and at least two people had to memorize a bible verse. The length of the Bible verse depended on your age. After reciting Bible verses we would sing classic kid songs like "Zacchaeus was a wee little man" and "Father Abraham". Then we would separate into three groups: Choir practice, arts and crafts, bible study. We would rotate through each group every Sunday. Two to three lucky (or is it more appropriate to say "blessed"?, I'll stick with lucky) children were selected to help bag cookies. The lady in charge of Sunday School also worked at the local cookie factory and brought us boxes and boxes of cookies. Every Sunday it would take at least one hour for the small band of children to bag up cookies for all the children in children's church. Of course, if you were bagging the cookies you got to eat cookies for an entire hour, plus you took home a bag of cookies bigger than others. My favorite cookies were the animal cookies covered in pink frosting with colored sprinkles.

As we got older and moved beyond the chapel, our church offered programs for teenagers. Our Sunday morning moved us from the chapel into another building on our campus, we called "Daniel's Den". It was a building with three floors that included lounge chairs, a kitchen, a pool table downstairs, fireplace, and a basketball court outside. This is where young people could congregate on Sunday. There was the youth and young adult choir, the dance team, the step team, the drummers, the basketball team, youth deacons, youth ushers, and a few more I cannot remember. We would have one or two Sundays each year that was dubbed "Youth Sunday" and the entire church service would be handled by teenagers. From the opening prayer and scripture, to the praise and worship selections, the raising of the offering, and the sermon and benediction. We were being trained so that we became older we would not depart from God's ways. We were also being strategically placed with others who shared our common belief system and inherently created a support system for each other.

Don't play with fire

The youth ministry would also hold overnight events. Unlike our church's shut-in prayer services that would consist of prayer and singing, our overnight event was a party. Food, lots of food, lots of good food. Some music and games to play. Of course, they had to force us to sit down at some point and read some Bible scriptures and learn something – but I don't remember that being the focal point of the night. To be honest, my fondest memories of preparing for that night was thinking about which girls would be there and how I could maximize 14 hours to make one of them my girlfriend by the morning. (Wait, how was this possible? I was trained up right in church, destined to be a child of God – how can I be thinking about premarital sex and promiscuity at such a young age?)

I hope you picked up on the sarcasm oozing from my fingertips. My hormones were raging out of control in my teenage years. My friends were all doing "it" (or talking about doing "it"), my mom offered me just enough freedom to make "it" happen. I was out of control, making a lot of adult decisions with a childish mind.

One time during our overnight teen session. we were having a discussion about sex. This was heavy, okay. We were in the late 80's and the word "sex" did not come up often in church. Definitely not when talking with children, it was best to just assume that was not happening, could not happen, never happens. So as the conversation grew, I became more and more interested. I started asking real questions about how to stifle a natural desire, almost admitting that I was engaging in this behavior. Then one of our friends spoke, he said something so simple, yet so powerful. It still sticks with me to this day, and I can vividly remember the scene around me when he said it.

We were lying on sleeping bags on the floor downstairs. It was cold, but not uncomfortable. I was leaning up against the wall towards the back of the room. This friend who was about one year older than me, said "If you don't play with fire, you can't get burned. I don't put myself in situations where I can be tempted to have sex. If I am in the room with a girl and we are kissing and stuff and it is starting to get heavy then I stop. I get up and walk out because I know that if I stay there too much longer then I will do something I am not supposed to do."

Full disclosure – my reaction at the time... "Oh snap, he's a virgin" ...let the jokes fly. My reaction years later... "Oh snap, this guy had it right way back then." We have to understand our temptations and work vigorously to avoid situations that feed into those temptations.

This is the same situation that Joseph found himself in when Potiphar's wife propositioned Joseph. To recap, Joseph was set up to be murdered by his brothers, but at the last minute his life was spared and he was instead sold into slavery. He ended up working in the house of Potiphar. Joseph is described as well-built and handsome, and the wife of the house noticed. She tempted Joseph to commit adultery day after day, but Joseph refused. One day, the wife caught Joseph by the cloak and attempted to lure him to bed, Joseph was in such a rush to flee from temptation that he left his cloak behind. This forgotten item served as false evidence that put Joseph in prison.

There are other instances in the Bible that encourage us to "flee" from sin: 1 Corinthians 6:18 – flee from sexual immorality; 1 Corinthians 10:14 – flee from idolatry; 1 Timothy 6:11 – flee from ungodliness. The Bible is clear – the best way to resist temptation is to remove ourselves from its presence. And not backing out slowly with your pointer finger in the air – just flee!

Sin is good

For all have sinned and fallen short of the glory of God. We all know sin is a bad thing and we work so hard to do the right thing – so why do we sin? Why do we sin on a daily basis? I can tell you why, because sin is good. Pick your sin, go ahead pick your favorite sin.

I'll start with fornication. The Bible is pretty clear about the dangers of engaging in premarital sex. We are intertwining our spirit with another person's spirit – and now we are forever connected in the spiritual realm. I do not know that person's upbringing, their struggles, their addictions, challenges, hopes, dreams, failures, friends, enemies, etc. And now, if I happen to run into that person 1 month, 2 years later – their baggage can now become my baggage. This is why it is better to be patient and careful about who you choose to lie down with sexually. I would much prefer to be in an intimate spiritual relationship with only one other spirit in this world – or at least keep that number as low as possible. But nevertheless, we engage in premarital sex. People inside and outside of the church do it. Careers are lost over this desire. Families and homes are destroyed over this desire. Lives are lost over this desire – so why do we do it? It feels good.

We enjoy the physical and emotional joys sex brings. We enjoy the feeling of knowing that we have been chosen to be special, to be let into someone else's world that is restricted. It may feel bad in other ways, but in the moment it feels good.

Let's try another sin: gossip. We spend time talking about others entirely too much. There used to be a 30 minute show that would come on the television every day devoted to celebrity gossip. Well now, there are entire channels devoted to providing 24 hours of gossip. There are also social media outlets and influencers that make millions of dollars by simply talking about other people and their lives. I don't blame them though – I blame you who engage with them. We are the ones who are tuning into this garbage, which then opens the eyes of the companies who want to sell us things. The companies pay these outlets and influencers money to advertise to us – the person who owns the channel becomes a millionaire, the person who owns the company who advertised to us becomes a millionaire, and the consumer (the one who ate the gossip and bought the advertised products) suffer financially and emotionally. So why do we do it?

Gossip is fun! I'd much rather hear about someone else's problem than talk about my own problems. I know my problems very well, and I can only assume they must be worse than others because other people are seemingly always smiling and laughing every time I see them. I am also game to talk about someone who talked about me. I usually don't want to tell other people's business, but if you violated my trust then I don't mind violating your trust. And the cycle continues.

My point is – we don't sin because it is bad. We sin because there are benefits we accrue from engaging in this behavior. I am learning to work less on stopping the behavior, and work more on understanding why I am engaging in that behavior. There is something missing in my life that I am trying to fill with this behavior, which is leading me to engage in sinful acts. And these sinful acts, pull me further and further away from my relationship with Christ. Each time I sin, I break the relationship.

The company you keep

Fast forward a few decades, now I am leading the youth ministry at my church. One Sunday I shared the story about King Rehoboam in the Bible. Rehoboam was the son and successor of King Solomon and the grandson of King David. Before King Solomon's death, the kingdom of Israel was already disintegrating and when Rehoboam began his reign there was plenty of friction in the kingdom about separating. There was so much turmoil and Rehoboam did not know the best course of action. He visited the elders who served his father, who advised him to listen to the people. King Rehoboam then consulted with his friends he grew up with who advised him to tighten his grip on the people and make them do as he commanded.

King Rehoboam decided to listen to his friends, instead of the elders and suffered greatly because his kingdom ended up being divided into 10 different tribes. They essentially ran the king out of town, and when he returned he was only left with one tribe, Judah, to reign over. We have to be careful of the company we keep and the people we let into our lives to seek counsel. On the reciprocal side, we have to be prayerful when others come to us for advice and ensure we are speaking from God's perspective and not our own selfish ambitions.

There is a saying that you are the average of the five people closest to you. Well that is not entirely true because the network extends to more than five people, but let's stay with that notion for now. The five people closest in your life will influence you in ways you cannot imagine. If those five people love horror movies, you will watch and come to enjoy horror movies. If those five people, value prayer and fasting, you will learn to value prayer and fasting. We all have to take a hard look at the lives of those around us and see how our lives are mirror reflection of them.

I can offer two suggestions that have helped me reduce distractions by fleeing from people who have negative influences. One, have the courage to remove negative people from your life. Let go of those relationships that are toxic, judgmental, and negative. This will free up room to add a friendship that helps you blossom, and that offers support either verbally or non-verbally – an opportunity to learn or teach or (ideally) both. Here are six specific steps to take to maintain healthy friendships:

- Stay away from chronic complainers
- Stop participating in meaningless conversations.
- Share your ideas only with people who are supportive or willing to provide constructive criticism.
- Minimize your interactions with "friends", coworkers and family members who are negative, discouraging, drama stirrers and bitter.
- Stop watching television shows that emphasize drama and stop reading negative posts on social media.
- Surround yourself with positive and successful people

Finally, look for people who share the same values as you do. If Christ is truly the head of your life, then you want to be around people who hold that same belief. This does not mean that every interaction will be a prayer and tarry session – it does mean that every interaction will happen with an understanding that "if God is not in this, I don't really want to do it". And that is the guide post for a true relationship with Christ.

Chapter 11 – Start small and gradually increase...Spiritually

"Though it is the smallest of all seeds, yet when it grows, it is the largest of garden plants and becomes a tree, so that the birds come and perch in its branches"
-Matthew 13:32

ost Christians and even non-Christians know that Jesus is considered a miracle worker. From His first miracle of turning water into wine at the wedding reception, to walking on water, healing the sick, raising the dead, feeding 5,000 with two fish and five loaves of bread, causing the lame walk and allowing the blind to see. Where we falter is understanding the depth of the lessons embedded within each miracle. In John 9:6-7, the story is retold of how Jesus healed the blind man. Jesus spat on the ground to make mud with His saliva, then He put the concocted mud on the blind man's eyes. Jesus then told the blind man to go and wash in the Pool of Siloam. The blind man went and washed, and then he was able to see for the first time.

This familiar story from the New Testament may raise questions about why Jesus did not just pronounce the blind man healed and send him on his way. This was His approach with the women with an issue of blood, and it did not require a (let's be honest) a gross process of mixing saliva with dirt and smearing it on a man's face.

Commit to reading one scripture a day, or one chapter a week. Then you can gradually increase to one chapter a day, or one book a week. Celebrate the small victories.

It requires less than you think

Is it possible Jesus healed this blind man in this manner, in the way He did so that the man could also play a small part in his healing? This way gave the man an opportunity to receive that healing by taking one small step of obedience, he heeded God's command to "go". During this Bible passage, Jesus makes it clear to His disciples that the man had not been born blind because his parents had committed sin, but so that God would be glorified through the work Jesus did in healing him. This is one example of a miracle that is chock full of lessons about how God uses people's situations to bring glory to Himself, about how He chooses to do His work, and about spiritual blindness and sight. But it also gives us this important truth – when God is in the midst of doing something wonderful – even miraculous - He may asks us to take some small steps toward making it happen. We have to pause and ask ourselves what miraculous thing is

God prepared to do in our lives and are we willing to be obedient and play a small part in our blessing?

I have never been a perfect Christian. I have made, and continue to make many mistakes in my faith walk with Christ. I would like to think I make less mistakes now that I am a more mature Christian. More importantly, I know who I am in Christ and I am comfortable with myself. When I was in college, I was extremely confident - quite handsome and witty – but I was not comfortable with myself and I did not know who I was in Christ. I struggled between the desires to fit in with the crowd, chase shiny things (cars, clothes, women, trends, etc.) and live the life I listened to nearly every Sunday from the choir stand. My point is – I made a lot of mistakes. And not the mistakes in shut closets behind closed doors – mistakes that were broadcast for everyone to see.

Nevertheless, I was still revered as a "good guy". There was always something about me that others could see that separated me. One evening I was talking with a friend in her dorm room. The evening turned into night and the conversations became deeper and more personal. I was secretly hoping this late night conversation did not turn into "something else" because I genuinely was not sexually attracted to her and I was enjoying the conversation. (Spoiler alert, it did not turn into anything sexual – this is not where the story is heading).

As we were sitting on her bed she started to open up about her hesitations with church. She retold me a few stories about how she grew up being taken to church and was always captured by the raw emotions that happened during the church service. She almost had tears in her eyes as she talked about the feelings she was remembering. Then, she contrasted that with the behaviors of the people around her after church was over. She told story after story about how people from the church hurt her and her family – which built a wall of distrust around those church members and eventually the institution those church members were associated with – the church.

She asked me why I went to church so often and why I seemingly carried myself differently than my other fraternity brothers.

I began to open up and share with her about my experiences with Christ. I had never spoken to anyone on campus this candidly about what my spiritual walk meant to me. As we spoke, at times it felt like she was not even in the room and that I was verbalizing to myself why my walk with Christ is so important. This was the spiritual awakening happening in my life that evening. (Let me pause the story to emphasis this was not the day I put away childish things. It did not take long after this long conversation into the early morning for me to get back to my old ways).

Then I did something I rarely do (even to this day) – I asked her if we could pray. She was hesitant at first, but eventually she agreed to let me pray for her. I prayed that God would reveal Himself to her in a real way, to demonstrate His existence and His love for her in a manner that would be indisputable. After we prayed I then asked her to do something. I said, "You should get a Bible, and you should start reading it." I could not point her to a specific chapter or book or scripture, instead I said she should just take one small step. I said with all the conviction I could - "I know that if you take one small step towards God, He will take two big steps towards you".

I wish I could wrap this story up with an amazing testimony of how she is a pastor or is raising the next praise and worship leaders of our generation. But honestly, I have no idea what she is doing now. In fact, we never had another one-on-one conversation about Christ or really anything. I do not know if she took that "one small step" or if God revealed himself to her in an indisputable manner. I can even barely remember her first name, and it would take some serious digging to find her last name.

Here is how I can wrap up this story – that conversation was life changing for me. I often think about it in the context of how quickly that late night encounter could have going in a completely different direction. It is not often that two college students, whose social interactions centered around fraternity parties, would spend four hours sitting on a bed talking about Christ.

Air mattress make billions

Brian Chesky, Nathan Blecharcyzk, and Joe Gebbia are the co-founders of Airbnb, a $31 billion company. Brian, Nathan and Joe started small and gradually increased. Airbnb started as an idea to earn a few extra bucks so they could continue pursuing their other business ideas (one idea was a cereal company called "Obama O's" – sounds tasty). The year was 2007, and roommates Joe and Brian could not afford the rent for their San Francisco apartment. They realized there was a designers' conference coming to San Francisco, and they knew hotel prices skyrocketed during conferences.

It started with an email from Joe to Brian, suggesting they rent out some air mattresses to conference attendees. They could spice up the experience by offering breakfast in the morning, a workspace, and free Wi-Fi internet. They even offered to serve as city tour guides for the designers attending the conference.

They created a simple website: airbedandbreakfast.com. They purchased three air mattresses and laid them down in their apartment. Their first guests paid $80 to stay on the air mattresses. After that simple cash influx, Brian and Joe realized this could be bigger. The connected with their old roommate, Nathan to build the business. They were really digging the idea of an Air Bed and Breakfast.

The second time they launched, at the SXSW conference in 2008, they only had two customers, and Brian was one of them. Later that year, they had accumulated eight rejections from angel investors and seven investors did not even bother to call back. The next big launch was in December 2008 at the Democratic National Convention in Denver. This time they decided to market their Air Bed and Breakfast idea by selling Obama O's and Cap'n McCains cereal boxes for $40 each. Each cereal box included information on Airbnb, and they netted approximately $30,000.

In 2009, the founders participated in a prestigious startup accelerator and after a few more rejections, they received a $600,000 seed investment. Four years later, the company boasted rentals available in 89 countries and one million nights booked on the platform.

From a glamorous air mattress rental to a website platform. It started small.

Just try it

A common refrain to hear me say is – "It is never the right time to get started, so just get started now." People will always point to tomorrow when the day is fresh, next week when the current tasks are done, next month when this project is done, next year when they finish school, or in three years when baby girl graduates. The reality is that tomorrow, next week, next month and next year – there will always be some other excuse or impediment to getting started.

It does not have to be a full time commitment. It is about starting somewhere and then allowing God to unlock the mysteries of His Word in your life. By committing to reading one scripture or daily inspiration a day, you will find there is something that enhanced your day. You read something that spoke directly to your situation you were currently facing or did not even realize you were going to face. That revelation wills you towards wanting to know more.

I am a picky eater. Well that is what my wife says. I would rather describe myself as someone who knows what he likes and what he doesn't like. My food tastes are pretty simple: I want to eat something I ate before. I'm sort of beyond that stage in my life where I am up for trying new things. I have seen a lot and done a lot, I'm good.

I find myself at house parties and there is a weird-looking dip on the table. The dip was prepared by someone I like and trust, and they approach me and say, "Hey, did you try this dip - I made it". Lie #1 – I'm not really that hungry. The response: "Oh, this isn't filling but you should really try it. I mixed in paprika and sour cream". Excuse attempt #2 – "Does it have eggs in it, I don't eat eggs". The response: "Oh no, I used some mayonnaise, but you can eat that right?". Now I am in an awkward position between being a jerk and just saying "No, I'm too bullheaded to try new things" and simply tasting it. I choose the latter. I scoop a small amount on sampler plate and then cover the plate in chips. I can always eat chips. I scoop a small amount of dip onto the chip and cautiously place it into my mouth. The flavors explode in my mouth. Wow, this is really good. Was it just a fluke though? My friend is staring at me gesturing with a nodding head and an expanding grin. I take another chip and add an even more generous portion onto the chip – this time I open my mouth with anticipation and I am left satisfied. I reach for the serving spoon and add more dip onto my sampler plate. My friend walks away satisfied, and so do I.

This is our approach to most things – we start out small. Let me try it. Once we have a taste, we begin longing for more. If this is our experience with some strange-looking dip on a potluck table – what would our experience be with coming back into communion with the creator of this world, the redeemer of our sins, the comforter of our soul? We will eventually find that we cannot get enough.

Chapter 12 – Educate yourself...
Spiritually

How much better to get wisdom than gold, to get insight rather than silver!
- Proverbs 16:16

Commissioned, the Winans, John P. Kee, Vanessa Bell Armstrong – these are the artists that influenced my current musical taste and laid the foundation for my faith. My Mom only played gospel music in her Red 1986 Isuzu. Even more, she would pick one cassette tape and play it over and over again. The Isuzu had this 'fancy feature' where the cassette tape would automatically flip itself over at the end, so my Mom didn't even have to eject and reinsert the cassette. (The one time I recall my Mom deviating from gospel music was when we listened to the Whitney Houston album on a long road trip to Los Angeles. I remember being so confused and wondering whether she "backslided"). This infusion of gospel music throughout my entire childhood years ended up giving me a false sense of my faith and commitment to Christ – and when it was tested in my high school and college years (and let's be honest through my early adult life also) I did not receiving passing grades.

Study the word of God for yourself, read the history and teachings of religions and faiths different than your own

Ordinary just won't do

To this day, I herald Commissioned as my favorite music group (barely beating out New Edition). My favorite artist is Fred Hammond (barely beating out Bobby Brown). Whenever I hear a song from Commissioned, it just takes me back to a simpler time in life. One powerful song I heard at least 4,000 times goes like this:

> "Have you ever needed someone, a shoulder just to cry on, to ease the agony, and find tranquility?
>
> "A sweet gentle touch, that speaks soft words of love that mean so much
>
> "The ordinary just won't do, I need someone that's pure and true
>
> "I can always find it in you Jesus"

Wow, what a powerful and simple stanza. What I heard over and over again is that sometimes you can't rely on friends or family – sometimes you need the spiritual encouragement that only comes from the Holy Spirit. There will be times in your life when your best friend won't be able to console you, and that is when you can turn to Jesus for strength. Can I share one more stanza?

> "Lord I need a special touch, that will mean so very much
>
> "Close friends they don't seem to understand, problems in your life so complex who can comprehend
>
> "Tragedy when you need relief, only Jesus Christ can supply your needs

I would sing those lyrics mostly on key and definitely on beat. But you know what? I had no "close friends", no problems in my life that were "so complex", and had not experienced "tragedy" significant enough to know that only Jesus Christ can supply my needs. I heard I needed an extraordinary relationship with Christ, but I never exercised that right. Until tragedy struck!

Tragedy strikes eventually

I lived through a very messy and painful divorce. We fought over money, property, investments, debt – but what hurt me the most was the fight over our two children. I did not have the opportunity to grow up with Mom and Dad in the same household, and it pained me to know that I was not going to offer that benefit to my son and daughter.

There was so much drama every time we visited the courthouse – the judge gave an order and rescinded the order, the bailiff needed to break up a near fight in the court room, I hired and fired two attorneys and decided I was the best person (and most affordable person) to represent myself during the divorce hearings. I always share this astonishing fact that our divorce case took almost as long as the marriage lasted. I had finally seen tragedy strike in my life.

While I was managing through a divorce, my employer decided it was time for me to move on. They respected me enough to "let me resign", but it was my first and favorite (still) employer. I could hear Bishop Hezekiah Walker singing the declaration that God would not put more on us than we can bear. But the powerful voices of his choir was not going to be enough to get me through this. I remember praying to God and telling Him, "I think you may have confused me with someone else – I am not as strong as you think. I don't think I can handle this".

The Cathedral of Christ the Light Church was erected in Oakland, California adjacent to Lake Merritt. The church was opened in 2008, and they broke ground in 2005. The church is located near the Alameda County courthouse I had to visit too often for divorce proceedings, mediations, filings, etc. I would always leave the courthouse, turning left towards the lake to walk back to my car simply dejected and mentally beat up – wondering how had I found myself in this horrible situation. I was not a bad person, but I was living through a really bad scenario. I would look past the lake and see the Cathedral of Christ the Light church, well there wasn't a church it was big hole in the ground.

It is also worth noting that this church was being built on the same parking lot of the building where I first started working – the firm where I had resigned from. I had parked my car there so many times and spent lots of hours in that building. So I really was not just looking at the hole in the ground – I was looking at the building and reminiscing when life was so much predictable and I felt so much more successful. Then I would look down the building and see a big hole, a big mess in the ground. This was a mental exercise I would replay every time I left the courthouse. I could not help thinking that the big hole in the ground was a representation of the big hole in my life. I repeated this exercise and mental thought process for about two years.

One day I was leaving the courthouse after another tough day, and I looked at the building and then fixed my eyes over the lake towards the church construction but instead of seeing a hole...I saw the frame of a beautiful building. It felt like the frame had shot up practically overnight. One day it was a hole, and the next day it was the framework to a work of beauty.

It was in that moment I heard God speak to me – as clear as ever – and say "It takes time to build something beautiful. I needed to build your foundation so when I showed you to the world I knew you would be able to stand". I realized I needed to be broken down, and rebuilt from my foundation in order to build a work of beauty that will withstand natural disasters. I have never looked back.

Building my foundation

I make an intentional effort to know God for myself and educate myself. When a pastor or preacher reads a scripture, I research to understand the context of the scripture. What was going on with the author of these scriptures before he wrote this, what was challenging him, who was chasing him, what battle did he just win, what failure did he just suffer? I gradually became less reliant on what I heard and more reliant on what I learned.

I have visited fancy restaurants with pre-fixed menus, I don't care too much for them. While it is an interesting experience, I prefer to be in control of what I eat. That also holds true for church services. If I just accept what the pastor, preacher, evangelist says without researching it and studying it for myself – I am just eating what they presented. Don't get me wrong, the food I eat from fancy restaurants' pre-fixed menus taste good, very good. The combination of flavors and texture are amazing. Similarly, I have heard some amazing sermons that have spoken directly to me and tasted good. But in order for me to truly apply it to my life for powerful and sustaining change I need to study it again for myself.

I was building my foundation. Over the years, I have met other tragedies and complex problems but I know the Word of God so much better now that I have been anchored. It is going to take more than a job loss, or disrespectful look from a stranger to move me from my faith. I liken it to a ship that has a strong anchor planted deep in the soil of the seabed. Doesn't matter how strong the waves are rocking and the winds are blowing – I am not moving. I am not fearful that I will move.

Bond discounts and bond premiums

The most difficult concept to comprehend in the basic accounting class is amortization of bond discounts and bond premiums. It is so difficult my colleagues choose not to cover it. I took my basic accounting class during my college years – and I didn't get it. But I passed the class. I took my upper division accounting classes and bonds topics came up again. Uh oh. I did my best, I still didn't get it. But I passed the class. After my first few years of working in the accounting industry, here comes bonds. Uh oh. I somehow convinced my boss that I understood enough and he agreed to finish my incomplete work product. Another missile adverted.

Fast forward to my first time teaching basic accounting and the chapter on bonds came up. I resolved I was going to stop glossing over it – I was going to learn it. I read the chapter over and over again. I took feverish notes. I liked my lecture notes, I had some good jokes to tell – I had my calculations down. On the day I lectured, my palms sweated, my underarms sweated, my words stuttered, the eyes of the students were glazed over - I completely bombed. I knew it, they knew it. I could say that I learned much more about bonds than before, but I still did not 'know it, know it'.

The very next semester, I dreaded that chapter on bonds. I thought about skipping it but decided I would do better and I sat down to study and revise my lecture notes. This time I took a different approach. I thought *how does bonds relate to my life and my students' lives*? How can I make this relevant? Once I was able to answer those questions - I gave an amazing lecture on bonds. When you meet me ask me any question about bonds (from the basic accounting class) and I will leave you feeling very comfortable about explaining how bond discounts and premiums are amortized on the income statement.

The difference between learning it in college, teaching it the first time, and teaching it now was I took it out of the textbook and applied it into my life. The same thing is true for the Word of God, we have to take it out of the Bible and apply it into our lives. When I study scriptures I ask how does this relate to me – something that I have overcame, something that I am struggling with, something that I am anticipating?

I have a question on the final exam that leads off with a mantra I say repeatedly throughout the semester "If you can't explain it to your momma, then you don't know it". We need to study the word of God enough that we can explain it to our momma (or whoever we believe knows us best in this world).

From Eden to Eternity

The Bible is a history lesson. I have seen history teachers share historical facts in such a way that it is fascinating and interesting. These amazing teachers connect the history from 400 years with the history from 200 years to current events. We need to tell the story of our Lord and Savior with passion and vigor, and connect it to current events. We can only present like this when we study to show ourselves approved.

The Bible is still relevant today. It explains how we got here, and what our purpose is. Anything that exists, has a purpose. When we apply the scriptures into our lives, we unravel the purpose of our existence. I am not referring to the existence of human kind – I am referring to the existence of you. The Bible gives us detailed tutorials on how to heal our hearts after disappointment and when we experience fulfillment in relationships. Two indisputable facts about life are: we need to open up and trust others and others will hurt us. We need to be prepared for these challenges and equipped with the skills to be resilient.

One caveat, however, is the Bible can easily be taken out of context and can be dangerously used to hurt people, disenfranchise people, and defraud people. God's Word is transformative and life-giving – so my antenna is always up when I hear God's words quoted as a condemnation or criticism. This is when I can turn to my own understanding of the scriptures, to consider the Bible as a whole. It is my prayer that you also have a stronger comprehension of the Bible for yourself.

PART III

LIVING FINANCIALLY HEALTHY

Chapter 13 – Do it first...Financially

The plans of the diligent lead to profit as surely as haste leads to poverty.
- Proverbs 21:5

ompound interest is considered the eighth wonder of the world. I'm sure you have heard this before – if not, we will cover what compound interest is later in this chapter and why it is so amazing. But first, what are the other Seven Wonders of the World? There have been various lists of the 7 Wonders of the World compiled over the years. The Seven Wonders of the Ancient World is the first known list of the most remarkable creations; it was based on guidebooks popular among Hellenic sightseers and included only works located around the Mediterranean rim and Mesopotamia. The number 7 was chosen because the Greeks believed it represented perfection and plenty, and it equaled the sum of the five known planets of the time plus the sun and the moon. The seven wonders of the world are: the Great Pyramids of Giza in Egypt; the Colossus of Rhodes on the Greek Islands; the Hanging Gardens of Babylon in Iraq; the Lighthouse of Alexandria in Egypt; the Mausoleum at Halicarnassus in Turkey; the Statue of Zeus in Greece, and the Temple of Artemis in Turkey. Ironically, there are at least 10 other things also billed as the "8th Wonder of the World":

- The Grand Canyon
- Andre the Giant
- King Kong
- The Taj Mahal
- The Astrodome
- The Terracotta Army

- The Empire State Building
- The Palm Islands of Dubai
- The Panama Canal
- The International Space Station

We will not be discussing these later in this chapter.

Set aside a percentage of your monthly income before paying any bills.

Fatten thy purse

I have read many books that I attribute to 'changing my life' – I should explain what that means when I say it. I have always thought my life was heading in a positive, productive trajectory (for the most part). So when I read a book that "changes my life" or take a trip that 'changes my life' - what I mean is that I have debunked a belief that I have carried with me until that moment or I am adding a new mantra to my mindset going forward.

In flight, an airplane rotates about the center of gravity. During flight, an airplane's weight constantly changes as the aircraft consumes fuel. The distribution of the weight and the center of gravity also changes. So the pilot must constantly adjust the controls to keep the airplane balanced. That sounds like our lives. As we fly through life, we are centered around spiritual beliefs and cultural traditions, but we are also consuming energy from other sources that distributes our balance. Similar to flying an airplane, we should always be making minor adjustments to our flight plan all with the same goal of reaching our ultimate destination. One book which served as a source of energy that distributed my balance and created a new mantra to my mindset is *The Richest Man in Babylon* by George Clason. It is crazy how this book was introduced to me.

I started teaching as a full-time college professor in 2015. My assignments for the first two years were accounting courses: bookkeeping, financial accounting, managerial accounting, software accounting. Stimulating courses (I really mean it) for sure, but I was longing to have a deeper impact with students. I noticed that our college did not offer a comprehensive course in personal financial planning. I thought this was absurd – clearly this is one of the most important skills for young adults to be introduced to. It does not matter if you are going to school to become an accountant, an engineer, an auto technician, a paramedic, a biologist, or a music teacher – every one of those careers will receive and pay money, and have the sole or co-responsibility for managing at least one household.

I started the trek of creating a new course on campus that would provide a holistic view of personal finance. In my fourth year as a college professor, I finally reached my goal and was able to teach a course in personal financial planning. I was so excited to teach this course and poured my heart into developing lectures, discussions and exercises that would stick. One activity I created was a list of books that I described as "changing my life". It was a short list: *Rich Dad, Poor Dad* by Robert Kiyosaka; *The Millionaire Next Door* by Thomas Stanley; and *Jesus' Terrible Financial Advice* by John Thornton.

One student who took the class gave me rave reviews. He and I had worked together in previous semesters when he took my financial and managerial classes. We had a mutual respect for each other, but I did not really come to appreciate him on a more personal level until we spent a semester in Personal Financial Planning. On the last day of class he recommended I read a book written in 1926: *The Richest Man in Babylon.* I did. I loved it. I can't say I learned anything new, but I did learn simpler ways to describe the basic techniques for personal finance. Mr. Clason presents seven cures for a lean purse and five laws of gold. His first cure for a lean purse is "Start thy purse to fastening". He suggests "for every 10 coins thou placest within thy purse take out for use but nine. Thy purse will start to fatten at once and its increasing weight will feel good in thy hand and bring satisfaction to thy soul". To translate: if you earn 10 bucks, only spend 9 bucks. How simple, how true.

Yeah yeah yeah

I am sure you may be thinking *yeah yeah yeah, I've heard that before.* I sure hope you have. So why are you not doing it? That is not a challenge, that is not a threat. It is an introspective question that requires some careful consideration.

Most people find this simple concept of saving first most difficult because they are frozen by financial fears. The financial fears of not having enough money to do what they have to do and what they want to do. The popular approach is to wait until the end of the month and then save what is left over. This is a nonsensical approach for many reasons.

One, you will never have enough. Let's just call it what it is. I drive a nice car and live in a nice house. I see others driving nicer cars and living in nicer houses and I want their stuff. I am constantly scouring the internet for the latest cars and features, and will almost cause an accident to stop and follow signs for an open house in a nicer neighborhood. I have enough, and it is not enough. I have accepted that and learned to be content with where I am. What happens if you do not have a "nice car" or a "nice house"? Well, if that is your goal just know you won't get there without launching some saving strategy (and winning the lottery or becoming a viral internet sensation doesn't count – the odds are stacked against you).

Two, you are more important than the people you owe. Let's consider the four basic needs: food, shelter, clothing, and transportation – and how we prioritize paying others above paying ourselves.

Food can be purchased and consumed at low or no cost. Indeed, there are food programs galore that can provide you with food to eat. I am not concluding the solution is to get on state aid or visit food banks each week. I am concluding we make choices to purchase the food we want to eat, and the level of convenience we want. The more convenient the meal, the more it costs (i.e., purchasing a plate of spaghetti from a restaurant is at least four times as expensive as buying the ingredients and cooking it yourself, resulting also in leftovers for days). The better the experience, the more it costs (i.e., a steak dinner at a restaurant in lower Manhattan is going to be four times as expensive versus the steak dinner at the downtown Las Vegas).

Shelter is a necessity, but do we really need a three-bedroom home? Do we really need a one bedroom apartment? Do we really need our own room? These are choices we make – to not have a roommate or share an apartment or live further from work. Obviously, we need to have a safe place to live, and depending on what city you live in, that won't come cheap.

You can't walk around naked. We need to wear clothes, but do we need the latest trends on our back? Again, it is a choice we are making to upgrade our wardrobe every season. We could find gently used clothes at a second-hand store, and I am not referring to the thrift store (although that is an option). There are websites, high-end consignment stores, outlet malls and many other places were we can look good without paying full price.

You can't walk around everywhere. Obviously we need some form of transportation. My transportation of choice is a car, a nice car. But it is a choice. I could also choose to not have a car and share a vehicle with my wife (I shudder at the thought). I could take advantage of the bus system in my county since there is a bus stop right at the corner of my block. I could purchase a bicycle and take advantage of our bike-friendly city. Heck, I could download an app that allows me to rent bikes or cars on a short term basis. I could rely on ride sharing for longer trips or rental cars (ironically there is a car-rental center within 3 miles from my home).

My point is these are all choices we make – and I am not here to judge your choices... because I don't want you judging mine. The fact is every choice we make, we are choosing to make someone else richer. The restaurant owner is in the business of providing convenience and an ambience, while making a profit to become richer. So when we choose to eat out, we are adding to that owner's wealth and dreams. The landlord owns the property to build wealth, and is relying on your rent to help pay her mortgage on the property. Every payment we make to the landlord or bank (if we own our home) is making them wealthier. Thanks! The clothing company is making a killing (let's just call it what is) by selling us t-shirts, jeans, and jackets. The more well-known the logo or brand, the higher the cost. Every purchase I make is helping some entrepreneur or stockholder wealthier. When I pay my car note every month, I am making the bank a boatload of money in interest.

The choice is simple – who are you more interested in making richer: You or the restaurant owner? You or the landlord? You or the designer? You or the bank? You or the shareholders of the cable company? You or the social media influencer that you are paying a monthly subscription for exclusive content about what exotic trip they took last weekend (with your money)?

Pay yourself first - and let everyone else fight over what is left.

Compound interest

As promised, let's talk about compound interest. This is when the concept of saving a percentage of your income (or fattening your purse) goes into overdrive. In non-technical terms: compound interest is the interest you earn on interest. Going back to the *Richest Man in Babylon*, the third cure for a lean purse is to "Make thy Gold Multiply" by learning to make our treasure work for us. Once you commit to saving a percentage of your income before paying any bills, then you have to diligently put that money somewhere that allows it to increase. Do not put it under your mattress, or in a coffee can buried in your backyard. Put it to work, and benefit on the power of compounding.

For simplicity sake, let's say you put your savings into an account earning a paltry 1% annual interest compounding monthly. You make $1,000 in January and decide to put away 10%, or $100 into this account at the beginning of the month. (Remember, the rest of your vendors and creditors are going to fight over the remaining $900 – good luck to them). At the end of the month you would have earned $0.80 ($100 x 1% x 1/12). Nothing too exciting. But in February you make $1,000 and put another $100 into the account at the beginning of the month. At the end of the month you would have earned $1.67 (($100 + $100 + $0.80) x 1% x 1/12). Big whoopee - you say? Well, you just earned $0.07 more than what you earned ($0.80 x 2), which is almost 10% growth on top of your 1% growth (i.e., interest earning interest).

In March, you make $1,000 and put another $100 into the account at the beginning of the month. At the end of the month you would have earned $2.51 (($100 + $100 + $100 + $0.80 + $1.67)) x 1% x 1/12). Well hold on, now you earned $0.11 more than what you would have earned ($0.80 x 3), another 7% growth. I know we are talking about small change, but we are also taking about over a small period of time.

If we continued this example of $100 each month at 1% annual interest compounded monthly, it would total $42,097.79 over the next 30 years. That is $11,738 more in interest you would have earned simply from compounding. If we instead increase that monthly contribution to $500, then the total would be $210,488.95. That is $28,690 more in interest you would have earned simply from compounding. Are you getting my drift – interest earning interest!

If we kept the contribution at $100 each month, but increased the annual interest to 5%, the total would be $83,672.64. (That is $38,672 more in interest). A $500 contribution at 5% interest is $418,363.19. (That is $229,363 more in interest).

The difference in all of this is you are allowing your money to make money and make more money. But it all starts by you first 'allowing your money to make money'. You have to set aside a percentage of your income and let it go to work.

Chapter 14 – Forgive yourself...
Financially

Therefore, if anyone is in Christ, the new creation has come: The old has gone, the new is here!
- 2 Corinthians 5:17-18

ate is a word I am taking out of my vocabulary. The word can be used as noun or verb, when it is used a verb you are describing a feeling and when it is used as a noun you are describing something. In both instances, the definition of the word includes the same phrasing: "intense or passionate dislike". I am a very intense and passionate person, that is a well-known fact. However, I choose to focus my intensity and passion on things that are productive: things I like, not necessarily what I dislike. There is a factoid that says it takes more muscles to frown than to smile (that is not actually true unless you take the least smile expression on the spectrum, i.e. a smirk and compare it to a more aggressive form of frowning). Nevertheless, I still choose to smile over frown and focus on things that are positive than negative. Notwithstanding all I just wrote, I *hate* owing others.

List all your debts and the reasons why you acquired the debt. Reconcile and accept your values.

I once heard debt described as "evidence of your past sins." That strong definition sat with me. Said differently, debt is a constant reminder of decisions that you made. If you made those decisions when you were in a bad spot in your life (let's just go on a vacation to take our mind off X, or let's just go for some therapy shopping or if I have this car then she will want me) then every time you look at that item you purchased or reflect on that experience you financed, it reminds you of what led you there in the first place.

Circuit City

I am a technology groupie. I make a lot of poor financial decisions buying emerging technology. Before Apple changed the world with iPods I had a Sony DiscMan, I had a Zune. I made the bold decision to purchase a 3D television, a 3D Blu Ray player, plus four 3D glasses - thankfully they came with two 3D movies. (Is 3D home technology still a thing?). I bought a first edition e-reader, black and green font and read the Invisible Man (because it was one of the few eBook offerings I was remotely interested in). And I can keep going on.

When I was a college student in the 1990s, the credit card companies were allowed to set up shop right on our campus quad and encourage students to sign up for credit cards. (Unbelievable, that our higher learning institutions allowed these financial giants to prey on unsuspecting children, but I digress). I was not so much interested in a credit card, but the swag was always a weak spot. From a t-shirt to paintball tickets to free food from Taco Bell. I would apply for a credit card at least 2 times a month. Thankfully, and mathematically, I was consistently denied. From my uninformed perspective, it was a winning combination for me – I would spend five minutes filling out the paperwork and I would walk away with something I wanted. Twenty years later I now understand my credit application was run through an algorithm and they considered my race, my income (or lack thereof), and the high number of inquiries. It was a no-brainer for the computer to conclude they should stay far away from a borrower like me. Good call!

On the other hand my cousin, who also attended the same college, was loved by the computer algorithm. He would receive almost any credit card he applied for. He had multiple credit cards with anywhere from $250 – $2,000 in credit limit. We were close – and he trusted me, so he decided to give me access to one of his many credit cards. The limit was $500. He told me to make sure I paid the minimum balance each month and everything would be fine. You know where this story is headed, don't you?

My first visit was to Circuit City, one of the largest electronic retail stores in the 90s. I wanted to get a nice stereo system for my car, affectionately dubbed "Blue Magic". The cost of the stereo plus installation came up to $240. Slightly less than half the limit on the credit card, and I knew I could easily pay that off. I presented the credit card and 2 hours later – I was jamming the latest hip hop and R&B songs on my new stereo looking left and right hoping some girls were noticing my fly ride and booming system. I also was reflecting on how easy that was. I didn't have to visit the ATM and clear out my bank account. I had a new toy, and I still had money in my pocket.

The next week, I was at the mall. I could do the math, I still had $260 left to spend on my cousin's credit card. If I purchased this new jacket for $40 it wouldn't matter. The next day, a $30 purchase, then a $70 purchase, then a $50 purchase. The end of the month came, and my cousin received the bill. He showed me what I owed, a measly $26 dollars for the minimum balance due. No problem. Here you go. I was starting to kick myself for not getting into this credit card game sooner.

The next month, $20 dollars here, $30 there – and finally I hit my cousin's credit card limit. The end of the month came, time to pay another $42 dollars for the minimum balance due. I didn't have it though. I could pay him about $30 and he could cover the rest. He politely asked for his credit card back.

The next few months, the balance kept getting larger, the minimum payment due kept getting larger – and I became less and less interested in paying it off. The excitement of the stereo, jacket, and other junk I purchased had faded. I no longer felt responsible for paying for something that did not bring me joy. Even worse, the credit card was not even in my name.

I did not mean to, but I contributed to my cousin's poor credit score – which had long-term implications for years in his ability to purchase a car, rent an apartment, and eventually purchase a home.

Enough is enough

You would think I learned my lesson on using credit cards, but I did not. I never had another credit card until I got my first corporate card. I was responsible initially, but that eventually got out of control as well. Then I applied for a second credit card and a third credit card. Then I purchased a new car and a house. At my worst, I had amassed $54,000 in non-mortgage debt:

- Student debt – $15,000
- Car loan – $11,000
- Credit card debt – $12,000
- Equity home loan – $14,000
- Corporate card – $2,000

This was out of control, and I could not tell you what I was purchasing. More importantly though, I could tell you why I was purchasing it. I had to do a value assessment and ask myself the tough questions about what I truly valued.

The first reason I purchased without purpose was the opinion of others. I had a good job, was making good money, and I needed everyone that I knew to know that. I demonstrated that by wearing new clothes, loud clothes (the larger the logo, the better). I visited the mall at least once a week with no agenda or intention. I just wanted something.

The other reason I purchased out of control: I was unhappy with myself. I was not satisfied with what I had accomplished because I was constantly comparing myself to others. This led to "retail therapy". Research has shown that making shopping decisions can help reinforce a sense of personal control over our environment. It can also ease feelings of sadness. A 2014 study from the Journal of Consumer Psychology found that retail therapy not only makes people happier immediately, but it can also fight lingering sadness.

The third reason I purchased willy-nilly was I did not have any well-articulated long-term goals. Of course, I wanted to be rich and put my daughter through college and buy a big house. But those goals were not well articulated. What does "rich" mean and when will I achieve it? What school does my daughter want to attend, what will the tuition, room and board, and supplies cost and when does this money need to be banked?

The combination of these three things lead me to spending more than I was making.

As of November 2020, the United States national debt was $27,203,384,382,939. That is $27 trillion. That is 27 trillion times, our elected officials decided to spend more than what we earned. It is hard to fault myself or fault any other US citizen for living beyond their means. We are simply following the examples of our elected leaders.

The US mantra is: If you see it, find a way to get it – now! Is it possible that the United States is also suffering from the opinions of other countries, a self-identify crisis, and lack of long term goals? Hmm.

The snowball effect

We have a crisis in our country. The average debt for Americans was $90,460 in 2018. Those aged between 18 and 23 had approximately $9,600 in debt, the millennials (aged between 24 and 39) had approximately $78,400 in debt. The age group with the largest debt was between 40 and 55, with $135,800 in debt. Baby boomers between 56 and 74 had $96,900 in debt and even our aging parents over age 75 had $40,925. The good news is there is a method to get out of debt.

Before we talk through a four-phased approach for getting out of debt, we first have to do a self assessment and evaluate why we got into debt in the first place. We then have to commit to changing our behavior and mindset to avoid falling back into the same cycle. Debt reduction is not a diet fad. It is a lifestyle change. Without taking this important step you will be primed to enter the rinse and repeat cycle. You will get yourself out of debt, and then find yourself back in debt. This is one of the hardest steps because it requires us to take an honest look at what our true values are and reconcile what we are comfortable and uncomfortable with accepting. Below are four phases to getting yourself out of debt:

First, you need to list all your debt. Who do you owe, why do you owe them, what interest rate are you being charged, when is the debt balance due and what is the monthly minimum balance due. Next to each debt, write down why you acquired this debt. There will be some valid reasons for acquiring debt, for example student loans debt is (or can be) a great investment. Also, financing a home can be considered a great purchase. But did you upgrade to a 5 bedroom when you were perfectly fine with a 3 bedroom? Did you acquire student debt to become a connoisseur of ancient Italian art (when you have never been to Italy)? Be honest with yourself.

Second, you need to create a cash management plan (aka, budget) to know how much money you earn each month and how much money you spend on your savings, essentials, and wants. You should have a leftover amount called "debt reduction". The aim is to get this debt reduction number as high as possible by managing your essentials and your wants. (Do not sacrifice your savings – reread Chapter 13). Let's assume you earn $1,000, place $100 in savings and plan to spend another $600 on needs and wants. This means you have $300 in debt reduction money.

Third, pay the minimum balance on all your debt. For example if you have five outstanding loans and each one has a $40 minimum balance then you would spend a total of $200. This would leave you with $100 of debt reduction money.

Fourth, apply the snowball effect – find the smallest guy in the room and pick on him. Take the remaining $100 of debt reduction money and apply that amount to the debt with the smallest balance. I know that sounds bad that you are picking on the small guy, but really do you want to challenge the biggest guy in the room? You will lose, or at least you won't feel like you are making much progress and you will risk giving up. Build up your confidence by taking down the smallest debt.

Once you finish paying off the smallest debt, now you are left with four outstanding loans with a minimum balance due of $40 each. This means you would spend $160 on the minimum balance, but now you have $140 remaining in debt reduction money. Don't get excited – find the next lowest debt out of the four remaining and put all the $140 against that outstanding balance until you knock that one out.

Are you getting it? Now you have 3 outstanding loans with a minimum balance due of $40, $120 in total minimum balance. You put the remaining $180 of debt reduction money against the next smallest. You are building up momentum by watching the debt wash away.

Once you are clear of each debt balance, go back and reread why you got yourself in that debt before. Be forgiving to yourself for your foolish ways, and commit to not making that same mistake again.

There are other methods to eliminate debt like refinancing and debt consolidation, but those methods are dangerous because it does not take away the debt it just kicks the can down the road. Plus, the fine print of some of those contracts is disgusting.

The book of Proverbs says that the borrower is always a slave to the lender. I have committed to never be a slave again to anyone. So I forgave myself, committed to a plan and executed it.

Chapter 15 – Be consistent...
Financially

Let us not become weary in doing good, for at the proper time we will reap a harvest if we do not give up.
- Galatians 6:9

emember the Showtime Lakers! This was the exciting run-and-gun style of basketball exhibited by the Los Angeles Lakers NBA team. Their reign was from 1979 to 1991, where they won 5 NBA Championships. You remember the stars: Earvin "Magic" Johnson, Kareem Abdul Jabbar, James Worthy, and Michael Scott. The name that typically gets overlooked when gushing over this amazingly talented team was their power forward, A.C. Green.

Make regular contributions to your savings, investments, and retirement accounts.

Iron man

A.C. Green won three NBA championships with the Los Angeles Lakers in 1987, 1988, and 2000. Less than 90 NBA players, or 2%, hold that distinction. A.C. was also named an NBA All-Star in 1990. Less than 450 NBA players, or 10%, hold that distinction.

Unfortunately, A.C. Green is most revered for his vow of celibacy. Throughout his entire NBA career of 16 years, he remained a virgin. There are tales retold by teammates of how they tempted him by sneaking naked women into his hotel. He describes himself as a devout Christian and never smoke or drank during his entire NBA career. He even refused to spray champagne for the cameras after winning the championship.

In actuality, A.C. Green's most impressive NBA statistic is not his abstinence from sex – I'm sure others have done the same (wink wink). It surely is not his three NBA Championships, many players can stake claim to that honor. (Lessor known NBA player Patrick McCaw has three back-to-back championships, winning two with the Golden State Warriors in 2017 and 2018 and one with the Toronto Raptors in 2019).

A.C. Green's most impressive statistic is that he played 1,192 consecutive games in the NBA. His streak started on November 19, 1986 in San Antonio and ended on April 18, 2001 in Miami. During those 15 years, he played for four different teams (leaving the Lakers in 1993 and returning back to the Lakers in 1999 for one season). In fact, throughout his entire NBA career which started in 1985, A.C. Green missed only three games during his second season. A.C. Green is the epitome of consistency.

Consistency is not sexy

If I had a nickel for every time someone asked me for investment advice, I'd have... well less than $200.00 (but hey that is still a lot of the same question). One time my cousin asked me to meet him at a restaurant in Downtown Oakland for a weekday lunch. This was an unusual request. He had a look of concern on his face, and with a furrowed brow he explained how he and his spouse were in dire financial straits and they needed some advice on how to better handle their money and make sound investments. I think he was expecting me to give him some stock tips based on my uncanny ability to read financial statements, or my genuine interest in the movement of the emerging economies.

I shrugged my shoulders, shoved a forkful of fried plantains in my mouth and calmly replied "Just get started today". I casually encouraged him to start by contributing $50 a month to an investment account to buy fractional shares of an index fund. I think he fell asleep while I was talking.

He acknowledged what I said with a "yeah, okay, right" and then asked me a more direct question. I don't remember the exact question but it went something like – I don't want you tell me what you tell other people, give me the real advice. I proceeded to tell him a story.

I had my first daughter at the tender age of 18, just one month before I turned 19. I was in college, I was broke, I was dumb with money (and most other things). I had no financial resources to even start thinking about her future. I could only think about how to make sure her teenage mother and I stayed off of government assistance. (Yes, that was my first goal – avoid welfare and food stamps).

Eventually, I graduated from college and so did her mother. My daughter was four years old then. I was out of college, but still broke, and still dumb with money. I had landed a 'good job' making very good money. I still did not have the financial resources to start working on my 4 year old daughter's future. It stayed that way until four years later when I was visiting a friend in New York. She told me I should start putting money away for my daughter's education. I told her I could not afford to invest right now. (I spared the details of the reasons: I need to buy clothes and other stuff to impress people). She told me that all I needed was $50 each month. She gave me the name of the brokerage firm to use. I was attracted to their motto: "Slow and Steady Wins the Race." Their logo was a turtle with running shoes. I bit the bullet, took a deep swallow and opened a brokerage account. I submitted the paperwork allowing the brokerage firm to automatically take $50 each month from my checking account.

The first month at the agreed upon date, the brokerage firm withdrew $50.00. When I realized the money was gone, I panicked. I felt like I was not going to be able to make my mortgage payment. I was used to spending everything I had and my bank account was running on fumes at the end of the month. I survived, somehow.

The second month at the agreed upon date, the brokerage firm withdrew another $50.00. I had another panic attack thinking I would have to resort to eating pork and beans from a can for the last week of the month. My bank account limped to the finish line. After the third, fourth, and fifth month, I settled into the realization that I was $50 poorer each month. At the end of the first year, I looked at the bank statement – about $700. That was a lot of angst over a small benefit. Yet, I persisted. By then I was used to not having $50, plus I was too lazy to reach back out the brokerage firm to ask them to stop.

Over the years, I opened up a second account for my daughter and contributed $75 each month. I experienced the same trend, in the first few months it was tough - and then I was used to having $75 less. 10 years later, my daughter's two accounts were nearly $10,000 – thanks in large part to compounding, coupled with an untimed growth in the stock market. Those two accounts, combined with her academic scholarships allowed her to finish her undergraduate degree with zero debt.

I think my cousin fell asleep again while I was talking. He did not heed my advice. That was about 4 years ago from the time I am writing this chapter. The stock market has nearly doubled since our conversation. That means that a $50 investment each month (a total of $2,400) would be worth approximately $3,400 now – that is a 41% return on investment. Now that is sexy.

Discipline is the key

Consistency takes self-discipline. The book of Proverbs says "a man without discipline is like a city with no walls". Consistency also takes a long-term approach to success. I do not prescribe to, nor endorse quick fixes or get-rich-quick schemes. I know that anything worth having is worth working for and waiting for. I remember those Heinz ketchup commercials in the 80s that would show a bottle of ketchup upside down hovering over a plump hot dog – it seemed like eternity for 30 seconds while we waited for the ketchup to come pouring perfectly out of the bottle, then we would hear the sultry VoiceOver, "Good things come to those who wait".

I always ask people, what are you investing for? If they tell me they are getting ready for their kid's college education which starts in three years I tell them 1) it is kinda too late – think scholarships, grants, or a community college and 2) it ain't going to happen. Any significant increase in your investment in three years is going to be mainly driven by luck. Yep, I said it. If you are investing in the stock market, whether it is a relatively safe index fund or a 'can't lose' technology stock – your impressive success in less than five years will be based on the unpredictable timing of the market.

Between 2008 and 2019, six of the 10 years saw more than 10% growth, two of the 10 years saw less than 5% growth, and two of the 10 years saw negative growth, the largest being a 37% decline in the stock market in 2008. The stock market is cyclical.

On average, the stock market gains 7% each year – so when you factor in the 32% growth in 2013 and the 31% growth in 2019, you will need some big losses to get back to that average annual growth of 7%. Consistent contributions leverages that volatility risk by taking advantage of the swings. When the stock market is rising – it may be time to sell some investments and repurpose them. When the stock market is declining, it is a great time to buy investments at a bargain price.

Imagine you drive to a big box retail store to buy a roll of toilet paper, and right when you were about to pick the item off the shelf the store clerk comes over and reduces the price by 30%. Are you going to change your mind and say – oh no, I'm not going to buy that now. Of course not, that is ridiculous. In fact, you may even want to buy two or three rolls of toilet paper. But what if there were 8 other people heading towards that same aisle of toilet paper and collectively you all saw the store clerk reduce the price by 30% and then everyone started leaving the aisle. But not just walking away, running in a frenzy (like hair on fire frenzy) from the toilet paper aisle – would you have the confidence to keep walking toward those rolls of toilet paper? Would you still want two or three rolls at the discount price?

Maybe I took that example too far - but that is actually what happens with the stock market. You started purchasing stock because you believed in the stock market, the group of stocks in the fund, the company itself - and then when the price dropped and everyone else started running – you ran also. Warren Buffett says be "fearful when others are being greedy and greedy when others are being fearful". Unfortunately, too many people follow the opposite advice.

This is why it is important to have a goal before you start investing. When I started investing $50 and $75 each month I knew the goal was for my daughter's college education. I knew my daughter was not heading off to college until 2011. I was not swayed when the market declined 9% in 2000, 12% in 2001, and 22% in 2002 because I knew I had a long way to go. I also was not overjoyed when the market increased 29% in 2003 and 16% in 2006. I still had another five years to navigate. I was quite thrilled when the market increased 26% in 2009 – just being honest.

Automatic deductions are key

The key to discipline is to set it and forget it. The reason why I was able to be disciplined for 15 years, and another 17 years with my son was because I set up automatic deductions. I took the responsibility from myself and gave it to the investment firm. I authorized the investment firm to transfer a certain amount of money from my checking account each month into a 529 plan or custodial account for my kids. I also authorized the bank to transfer a certain amount of money from my account each month into a brokerage account for my own investments. I also authorized my employer to withdraw a set amount of money from my paycheck each month (tax free, thanks Section 401(k) of the IRS code) and invest into stocks that are growing tax free (thanks again, Section 401(k) of the IRS code). This method is much easier than relying on your fleeting memory to sit down each month and transfer funds. Set it and forget it.

Well, not quite forget it. Set it and *increase it*. Once you get comfortable with contributing $50 each month, press in and increase the contribution by $25 to $75 each month. You will experience the same angst in the beginning but eventually you will get used to it. Then, when you get your next raise (whether it is an annual raise or a starting a new job) look at your increase and set aside a percentage of that increase. This is the advice from another great book I read called *"Don't Spend Your Raise and 59 other Money Rules You Can't Afford to Break"* by Dara Duguay. This is another book I herald as having 'changed my life'. It was published in 2002, I probably read it around 10-15 years ago. I had to visit amazon.com to remember the entire title, and I saw that it only had 3 reviews. Two five-star ratings and one three star rating. No wonder the average American has only $17,000 in their investment account.

Chapter 16 – Reduce distractions...
Financially

The average time it takes to complete an associates degree in the California Community College system is pushing six years. Associates degree is generally known as the 2 year degree. It generally has 60 units, which should take a full-time student 4 semesters to complete. However, most students do not enroll in 15 units each semester, or they register for 15 units and end up having to withdraw from some classes, or they enroll and complete 15 units of classes that do not count towards the associates degree. The majority of students who enter a community college have a goal of earning an associates degree and transferring to a 4 year university to earn a bachelors degree. Hold your breath...fewer than 40% of community college students earn a degree or certificate within six years of enrollment. This is not a phenomenon specific to California Community Colleges. For one reason or another, most people set goals and then get distracted from achieving those goals.

Manage your advertisement consumption and identify impulse behaviors.

Saturday morning musings

I grew up in the 1980s. Back then, we had one television set and it was in the living room. For about four years of that decade our actual TV sat on top of another bigger TV that no longer worked. We also had one VCR, the kind that opened up vertically and welcomed you to place the video cassette tape into the slot and then press down hard to close. I remember when we got our first remote. It was a wired remote with a 10-foot cord plugged directly into the VCR. The remote had one button with a play and pause feature. Oh, I had the time of my life positioning myself 8 feet from the second television and bulky VCR and just pressing pause and play.

There are upsides to having one television in the house. We all watched the same shows and it encouraged family discussions. We always watched Wheel of Fortune, a favorite game show of my Mom. We would see who could guess the puzzle first. I think my Mom would give us grace and let us win sometimes. We watched Good Times, Alice, and Differn't Strokes together. I still remember our intense discussion about watching out for strangers after the "to be continued" Differn't Strokes episode when Arnold and Dudley were lured from the comic book store to a man's house and were asked to take off their shirts.

The downside to having one television is the house is – we all had to watch the same thing. I was not interested in Dallas or Kojak, but I had no other option. Either endure the television program or go into my room and play with my hodgepodge of toys.

The one time when the kids in the house controlled the television was on Saturday morning. We would rise early and pour a bowl of no-name sugary cereal and sit crosslegged in front of the television and watch the Flintstones, Scooby Doo, the Justice League, and Transformers. Our command of television entertainment usually ended around 12noon or when we would attempt to run out of the house before being tagged to do some Saturday chores, whichever came first.

At quite an early age I began noticing something when watching television – the commercials on Saturday were so interesting. The commercials generally featured kids smiling, running and playing with the newest toys. For some reason I recall there always being some rainbow or something that would streak across the screen, or some asterisk that would fly into the screen to emphasize the toy is "new" or "improved" or "limited time only". The commercials also seemingly featured bubble gum, fast food, snack food, name brand cereal, and other things I would crave. I found myself as interested in the commercials, as I did in the show feature.

Conversely, when I was watching Golden Girls with my Mom I had little interest in the commercials about some medication, or panty hose or liquor. When the commercial came on that was my cue to finish the dishes or continue working on my homework.

One day I suddenly realized the commercials were geared towards the audience they thought was watching that particular show. I know this seems very obvious, but I was about 9 years old when I came to this realization. I then became fascinated by watching commercials to understand who the advertisers think are watching the show.

Fast forward a decade, I graduated from college in late May. I had a job lined up that started in August. I had two months of nothing to do. Literally, I had no plans. I watched a lot of daytime television, like Jerry Springer and other trash television for most of the morning while lying in bed. I would also watch the commercials. Even today, over 20 years later, the commercials that come on during the day are geared towards insurance settlements, car insurance for those with bad driving records, and trade schools. Who do they think are watching these shows? This one trade school commercial would make me livid every time – there was a trade school advertising how people could earn an accounting certificate in nine months. Then the commercial would split to someone in a dress shirt and tie shaking hands with a successful looking business owner. I could not stand that commercial because I had just finished five years of schooling to earn an accounting degree. I saw it as a complete disrespect for my hard work, but I digress.

Good advertisers don't advertise

There is a fight for your money – and you are losing. Good advertisers no longer have to advertise. We are subconsciously led to spend money on the things we like or have been trained to like. Our world is filled with algorithms, artificial intelligence, and data analysis and it is hard for us to compete.

I am a 40+ year old African American male who loves God, Star Wars, and basketball. I have purchased so much unneeded NBA merchandise based on an email subject lines. "The Warriors Win – Celebrate with 50% off". 50% off? *How can I pass on that deal – but I don't need anything – well I'll look anyway, it is just a click away.* 20 minutes later, I have wasted 20 minutes and $50 purchasing a hat and sweatshirt I never knew I "had to have". Certain websites have eased the purchase process further by offering to "save your credit card information" or allowing you to "pay with 1-click". These so-called conveniences are just further feeding into our subconscious purchasing decisions.

Look, I am aware of what the marketers are doing and I am still sucked into their nefarious ways. Whenever Disney sends me emails the featured product is some Star Wars merchandise, because they know that will catch my attention. One time I looked at the same email from Disney that my sister received – it was identical except the featured product was something from Lion King because they knew that would catch her attention. We are constant victims to their tricks and unfortunately we lose too often.

Marketing equals markup

I am blessed to drive a Tesla Model S. I purchased it brand new in 2017, and I continue to marvel at the technology of the car. It is truly amazing that the car I purchased in 2017 is not the same car I have now – it is better. The software updates have done some minor and major improvements that keep me on my toes and excited when I get the notification that I have an update waiting for me. I am not the only one mesmerized by Teslas. Many people turn their heads when driving on the freeway to get a glimpse at whether the driver is truly 'driving' or trimming his nails while the car travels effortlessly at 69+ miles per hour while hugging curves like a Nascar professional.

Even more fascinating is Tesla does not participate in traditional advertising. When was the last time you saw a Tesla TV commercial, billboard, or website banner ad pointing you towards purchasing a Tesla? You haven't, right? Instead Tesla relies on word of mouth, superiority of its product, emphasis on innovation, and of course, its eccentric chief executive officer, Elon Musk and his legendary tweets. (Can you even name the chief executive officer of Ford, Hyundai, or Mercedes?)

Nearly all companies participate in various forms of advertising or marketing. Marketing is the activity, set of institutions, and processing for creating, communicating, delivering, and exchanging offers that have value for customers, clients, partners, and society at large. The purpose of marketing is to generate revenue for a brand, company, or organization. Marketing costs money. Total marketing costs are between 5% and 12% of total revenue. Companies are in the business of making money, so it stands to reason: the more money spent on marketing, the higher the expenses, the higher the price of the product.

Let's assume a company has a profit margin goal of 20%, which means the company wants to earn $0.20 for every dollar sold before paying taxes. (Every company has a profit margin goal, that is how they attract investors.). The Company pays $35 for developing a product and getting it ready for sale. In this case, in order to earn a 20% profit, then the company needs to sell the product for $43.75.

Of course, the cost of the product is not the only cost the company pays. They need accountants, lawyers, executives, executive assistants, warehouses, delivery trucks, and on and on. Let's say those total costs calculate to be an additional $12 per product. Now the total cost of the product, plus other costs is $47. If the company still has a 20% profit margin goal, then the price of the product needs to be $58.75. That is an additional $15 you have to pay for the product.

Now, let's add the cost of marketing to the already-long list of additional costs. Let's assume the marketing costs calculate to be an additional $3 per product. Now the total cost of the product, plus other costs and marketing is $50. If the company still has a 20% profit margin goal, then the price of the product needs to be $62.50. The $3 in additional marketing costs results in $3.75 more added to the price of the product. Guess who is paying that additional $3.75? The consumer – me and you. So the next time you see that hilarious television commercial during the big game, just know your laughs will cost you later when you are at the grocery store.

Dogged social media

At the time of this writing, I do not have a social media account. I acknowledge there are many benefits to having a social media account and I willfully give up those benefits often. My daughter was awarded an "up and coming" young professional award from a magazine in Birmingham, Alabama. I happened to be responding to a message on my LinkedIn account (I guess that counts as social media) and I saw the post on my homepage (I think it is called a "feed" by the young people). I was overjoyed. I called her immediately to congratulate her. She did not reciprocate the same enthusiasm. She told me that award was six weeks ago – she had already accepted all the "attagirl" and congratulatory emails. She then said "Oh yeah, you don't have FaceBook – it was all over FaceBook". I had to remind her that I need personalized announcements, and that it was also good that I did not hear about it when everyone else did – because I was now extending her congratulatory season.

Another time, I was talking with a friend after a few months of being out of touch with each other and she was sharing with me how her family was doing and how they are "hanging in there". I thought to myself – I must have missed something... in fact that is what I said to her "Uh, wait, did I miss something?". She said "Oh yeah, you don't have FaceBook – it was all over FaceBook". She then proceeded to tell me her father passed away 4 months ago and the courage it took for her sister and brother to manage through the pain of losing a loved one and persisting onward.

Despite my awkward moments, I am resolved to avoid social media. I do not think I have the strength to avoid their Navy Seal methods of convincing me to purchase something – whether it be clothes, an experience, food, a musical instrument accessory, a gadget for my home, a keepsake for my son – they are constantly scouring my likes and dislikes and feeding me information that I will respond to. I am not 15 months old, I do not need someone to feed me. I will choose what I eat. I will choose what I purchase. I will choose how I spend my hard-earned (and let's be honest, sometimes easily-earned) money.

It is critical to know what you value and what your goals are – and be sure that you first set aside time and resources for accomplishing those goals. Do not fool yourself into thinking you are stronger than this media machine. Make wise decisions by limiting your social media intake and creating a limit on how much you will spend each month on 'stupid stuff'. Budgeting is key

I do not regret most of my purchases though, nor am I a condemning anyone who engages in impulse buying. It is fun, it is therapeutic, and it produces dopamine. Research shows that the brain releases dopamine in anticipation of a reward. The unpredictability caused by shopping online results in even more dopamine because it creates the anticipation of waiting for the purchase, as compared to purchasing it in the store.

I do not feel a sense of regret because I allocate a portion of my income every month to "stupid stuff". Yes, that is correct – I have a line item in my monthly cash management sheet called "stupid stuff" and my goal is to use those funds on impulse buys to produce a brief sense of excitement and anticipation when I am bored or having a bad day.

The amount allocated depends on how much I have committed to saving, investing, paying down debt, covering my four basic needs (housing, transportation, food, shelter), and other wants. When I do not spend my allocated amount it gets carried over to the next month, so what I don't 'waste' this month I can 'waste' next month. This is my defense mechanism to the ongoing barrage of advertisement and media influence I am receiving every day. To be clear, I budget for distractions.

Fight back

Now that we acknowledge there is a fight for our money, we need to fight back. Here are four strategies to avoid financial distractions.

First, identify what distracts you. I have already acknowledged mine. Your distraction could be a financial emergency, or it could be a desire to keep up with the Joneses. Whatever it is, be honest with yourself and your accountability partner. Whatever has distracted you in the past is priming itself to distract you again.

Second, redirect your attention on what matters. Write down your financial goal. Share this goal with your accountability partner and a few other close friends you trust. By regularly declaring your goal it makes you more dedicated.

Next, track your progress because everyone likes to taste success. Pay regular attention to your positive habits, reward your milestone achievements, and do not be shy in adjusting your plans that are outdated or no longer bringing you joy.

Finally, increase your security to avoid becoming derailed by financial emergencies. Keep it "100" (as the kids say) – and create a space in your monthly budget for "distractions" or "fun" or "play money". This will keep you from falling back into feelings of guilt and favor when the advertising and marketing monsters creep back into your life.

Chapter 17 – Start small and gradually increase...Financially

His master replied, "Well done, good and faithful servant! You have been
faithful with a few things; I will put you in charge of many things. Come
and share your master's happiness!"
Matthew 25:23

-

-

ap music took some time to grow on me. When
the rap game first took hold in the 1980s I was
into it – I was rapping along to "Friends" by
Whodini, "It's Tricky" by Run DMC, and "No Sleep Till
Brooklyn" by the Beastie Boys. Mostly, I was being
influenced by my two older brothers and their friends. I
secretly still preferred Commodores and DeBarge when I
got the boombox to myself. I gave rap music another shot
in high school. I am still a fan of Tribe Called Quest – the
entire "A Low End Theory" album. I rocked with Kid N'
Play (more the fashion and dance moves than the music)
and the smooth and debonair sounds of Father MC. But
again, I was likely influenced by my high school friends. I
was more partial to this "hot new group" called Boyz to
Men and all the New Edition spin off albums. By the time
I got to college, my musical choices were even less under
the influence of my friends, so when one of my boys let
me listen to the Chronic album by Dr. Dre, I immediately
dismissed it. I did not smoke weed (neither did my friend
at the time), so I told him it made no sense to even jam
this music in our cars. I still do not smoke weed, but man
I could have never been wrong. My friend had his hands
on a classic before it was a classic.

Commit to an amount aim to increase that amount each year by a certain dollar or percentage.

Fo schizzle my nizzle

After admitting I slept on the Chronic album for about 15 months, I opened myself up to more music in that genre. I was on Jay-Z's Reasonable Doubt probably before anybody in the Bay Area – that is definitely a hyperbolic statement, but I was hip to it before any of the people I knew and hung out with. Of course, I was a fan of Tupac. I found his emotions and storytelling so compelling. I listened to Tupac songs about his life in the streets and compared them to my life in the college hallways and in between downtown San Francisco buildings during my summer internships. I learned to listen more intently to the words and the many meanings behind the words. I also bopped to Biggie Smalls – I remember flying to Washington D.C. three weeks after his murder to party at Howard University. My friend from Oakland and I visited the record store across the street from Howard's campus to pick up the new Life After Death double CD released in March 1997. We were deathly afraid to let people know we were from the West Coast, living in some concocted fear that they would accuse us of Biggie's murder!

I was always partial to the Bay Area – and no one was representing the Bay Area harder in the 1990s than E-40, aka E-Fonzerelli, aka Forty Water. I first met E-40 at a television studio. A local radio station was filming a pilot for a new show and they asked my fraternity to be in the opening credits of the show and also kick off the show with a step routine. They had booked E-40 as the musical guest for the pilot. So here I am at the studio in the green room with about six other frat brothers and we are flexing for sure. Then, in comes E-40 – a large intimidating man by himself, with three other dudes who were as large, or larger than him. None of them smiled. It was a respectful head nod between our entourages, but not much else. I was thinking to myself *does this dude know who we are?* I guess I should have been thinking to myself – *dude, do you know who that is!*

Over the years, we had other run-ins with E-40 and his crew. He knew my fraternity threw the hottest college parties in the Bay Area, so the Click (B-Legit, D-Shot, Suga-T) would regularly come through.

I can quote lots of E-40 lyrics but the one that always stood out vividly in my mind came from the 1996 song, Rapper's Ball featuring Too-Short (another Bay Area legend in the rap game) and K-Ci (from Jodeci). The gist of the song is about ballin' out – showing off how much money you have. Definitely a goal of mine in 1996, which ironically led to some poor financial decisions. The song goes on and on about how much money they have and the brands they spend it on, the islands they visit and the parties they throw. The one bar that captures me to this day and has become one of my financial guideposts goes:
"Why [folks] can't be broke sometimes?
Sometimes it's cool to floss
But don't buy a eighty-five thousand dollar car
Before you buy a house"

It seems like every time I would hear those lyrics on my speaker system I would be serendipitously driving by an apartment building with a Mercedes sitting in the driveway. It was always a wake-up call – and it also begged the question - were they not listening to E-40?

SMART goals

We need to set goals, attainable goals. I am sure you have heard this acronym before around setting S.M.A.R.T. goals. I first heard this in the context of setting my annual goals at work, but it really resonated with me when I heard this acronym used in the context of setting financial goals.

SMART goals are – Specific, Measurable, Attainable, Relevant and Timely. Specific goals are well defined. Simply saying I want to be 'rich' is not a specific goal. Or saying I want to 'get out of debt' - again not specific enough. Those goals need to further defined as I want a 'net worth of $1,000,000' or I want to 'pay off all my credit card debt'.

Measurable goals have mechanisms to measure progress. How can you measure progress towards a goal of becoming rich? How can you measure progress towards a goal of having a 'net worth of $1,000,000'? The former goal has no measuring sticks of progress or regression, compared to the latter goal where you can calculate on an annual, monthly, weekly, or daily basis whether you are increasing or decreasing your net worth.

Attainable goals require you to stretch, but are not impossible. Imagine setting a goal of having at least $1 in the bank. That seems pretty easy to do – for most any American (whether you are working or not working, a homeowner or unhoused). Imagine setting a goal of having $10,000,000 in the bank. That is pretty difficult to do - and most Americans will not reach that. I do not want to go as far as to say it is impossible, but can I dare say... improbable. (There are 122 million households in the United States, and 1.3 million of those households are considered "Decamillionaires", the name given to those who have more than $10 million in the bank. That is about 1% of the US households.) You want to set goals that are achievable, otherwise you will grow weary because it sucks to keep losing.

Relevant goals are tied to your life's purpose. What if you had a goal of making a $1,000,000 a year? That is very achievable. But what if that goal does not align with your value system as a minimalist? You are not going to be committed to that goal because you have not defined or assigned what you plan to do with all that money. To quote another rapper I admire, Puff Daddy said "mo' money, mo' problems". Enough said, if you have it, you've got to spend it somehow someday on something. You won't stay committed to a goal if it does not align with your moral values and beliefs.

Finally, goals have to be time-bound. Many people have a goal of wanting to go on an exotic vacation one day – sadly those people do not get that experience. This is because these type of people have not sat down and said, "When do I want to take this trip and what is going to take to get the cash flow necessary to make that trip happen?" If the goal is set in some indeterminate future date, then you always have tomorrow to get started. If you really want to see that goal get accomplished you set a specific time frame – anywhere from 6 months to 18 months. If the goal date is more than 18 months, then you need to set sub-goals.

For example, I set a goal to pay off the mortgage on my investment property within five years. That is too long for me to stay focused, so I broke that goal down into annual goals. I need to pay off 15% in the first year, 20% in the second year, 25% in the third year, 25% in the fourth year, and then coast into my fifth year paying the remaining 20% off. Now I can measure my progress on an annual basis leading to the five-year plan.

Never give up

   Have you seen the poster of a frog being swallowed by crane? Picture this in your mind: There is a crane standing in shallow water looking regal and somewhat confused because something is in his mouth. You can only determine it is a frog in there because there are green arms protruding from the mouth of the crane with the green hands wringing the neck of the crane. At the top of the poster are the words "Never give up".
   I first saw that poster in the administration building at my college. I always found it comical, but I also saw the resolve in that image. It is not over until it is over. I used that picture to motivate a fourth grade basketball team I was coaching in a city league.
   Okay, the league commissioner set me up for failure. He can admit it now. My team consisted of my son, athletic but not fundamentally sound in basketball at the time, another kid, who was more athletic than my son but lacked any discipline, and six other kids who didn't know what dribbling the ball meant at the first practice. We had our first two spirited practices. Then we went into the gym for our first game. I had every intention on winning because I focused on emphasizing the players' strengths – our speed, our size. We were skunked. It was embarrassing. Game 2, Game 3, Game 4 – same results.

Great practices, horrible performances. It was clear the other teams just had better players.

So, I revised my goals. It was no longer about scoring more points than the other team for the game - it was about scoring more points in a specific quarter. It helped with morale, but even that was a goal we could not achieve with this band of misfits. So, I revised my goals again – let's focus on getting more rebounds than the other team. I would literally have a parent keep track of how many rebounds we got versus the other team each quarter. We would lose the game by 15+ points and be out in the courtyard celebrating because we won the rebound game in a couple of quarters. What I realized was that in order to win the game, you have to win at the little things. So I got the team to focus on the little things. The season was not long enough for all the little things to add up to the big things though.

We got to the last game and I was pretty excited. Apparently, I was not the only coach who was given the short end of the stick. There was another team in the league who was also winless, so we were going into a championship (of sorts) to see who would not have a losing season. I asked the team to focus on winning the rebounds game and just scoring more points than them in the first quarter. We were able to achieve both goals. We were outscored in the second quarter, but still competed well on the rebound tally. At halftime, we held a small lead. (At this point, I felt like the league commissioner should have just called the game since neither of us had ever felt this level of victory – not being blown out by halftime). I emphasized our small goals; rebounding, winning the quarter. We were successful in the third quarter and held onto that success for a nice easy win to the game. I probably should not admit this, but I was close to tears when I held up that image of the frog in the crane's mouth and told the boys "Never give up".

We did not get there by setting unrealistic goals, but by setting short, small achievable goals and then riding that success to the next slightly longer, slightly larger achievable goal.

When you think of financial success as a marathon, not a sprint, you realize it does not have to be made up in one stride. There are many strides that you need to take to reach the finish line.

On your mark

The challenge is deciding where to start and when to start. I can simplify that decision for you. Start now, start here. When I first put this thought into action it was difficult to identify a brokerage firm that would open an account for less than $1,000. I found one that allowed me to contribute $50 a month, but I had to commit to automatic withdrawals from my checking account. Ironically, that firm was owned and managed by an African American who understood the barriers to investing and created mechanisms to overcome those barriers by allowing for smaller investments.

Today, you can find apps, websites, and banking tools that will allow you to invest dollars, and less than one dollar, on a continuous basis. You can purchase fractional shares of individual stocks and funds by simply authorizing a bank to take the change from your purchase and move it into a brokerage account.

To be clear, this is not the preferred way of investing. It lacks true purpose and intent but it is a start. You do not need to wait until you have accumulated some magical number of $500 or $1,000 or $5,000. You can start right where you are. What you will find is after a few months of investing smaller amounts consistently, you will be embolden to invest larger amounts. Maybe you increase from $25 each month to $40 each month. Remember every dollar adds up (See Chapter 16).

Starting small also works in the derivative form. Let's say your goal is to eliminate debt, but you only have $50 each month to contribute to your $8,000 credit card balance. Start small and gradually increase. You do not have to wait until you have a $400 cash influx to make a big dent in your debt balance. You can start making small dents and trust me they will add up over time.

Gary Gilmore is heralded as the inspiration for the famous Nike tagline – "Just do it". In 1976 Gary Gilmore robbed a gas station, murdered the gas attendant and later murdered a motel worker in Utah. Gilmore was arrested and sentenced to death. Three months later, he found himself facing a five-man firing squad and they asked Gilmore if he had any last words. His reply was "Let's do it". Dan Weidman, the head of an ad agency heard those words from Gilmore and liked the "do it" part. The rest is history...I venture to guess that at some point in your life you have either said or worn the remixed words of a double murderer. So, I'll repeat it again - Just do it!

See how small ideas can blossom? Nike and its slogan are now a company worth more than $10 billion.

Chapter 18 – Educate yourself...
Financially

*Wisdom is a shelter as money is a shelter, but the advantage of knowledge
is this: Wisdom preserves those who have it.*
- Ecclesiastes 7:12

Discipule: *disce te ipse docere* - this is Latin for
"*Student: learn to teach thyself*". As a college
professor, this is my ultimate goal at the end of
each semester. I want to instill a hunger or desire within
each student to learn more about the subject I am
teaching. I am less concerned about students retaining
the information I shared on the five steps of revenue
recognition under generally accepted accounting
principles adopted by the Public Company Accounting
Oversight Board (yawn). I am more concerned about
students wanting to know the 'why' behind the increase
in revenues, and whether that reason is sustainable – and
lawful. When I am teaching the Personal Financial
Planning class, I aim to give the students the tools to find
answers rather than give them answers. Facts and figures
will fade from your memory, but experiences (like
researching the answer for your grandmother or reading
about an investment that yielded a 200% return) will
always remain tucked in the halls of your memory. To
loosely quote Cesare Pavese: we remember the moments,
not the days.

*Understand your investments. Why they make
money, and why they lose money.*

Just too fancy

I always enjoyed watching *In Living Color*, the skit satire show with Keenan Ivory Wayans, Damon Wayans, Tommy Davidson, and David Alan Grier. The show was also instrumental in launching the uber-successful careers of Jim Carrey, Jamie Foxx, and Jennifer Lopez (she was one of the Fly Girls in the first season). I would ensure I was home on Sunday nights at 8pm to watch all thirty minutes.

The skits were legendary – and even now when I see the show in syndication I will pause, watch and laugh like it was the first time I saw it. I would anticipate the joke, the surprise, the reveal, the absurdity. One recurring skit featured Damon Wayans playing the role of Oswald Bates, an incarcerated person with an advanced, but misguided, vocabulary. He would say things like: I propose to the population to present a predilection of purpose to preview, uh excuse me, protract the perfected plantation of our planet. In other words, eat less meat.

Keenan Ivory Wayans noted this character represented "every black man who thinks he is educated". I found it hilarious because I knew many people like Oswald Bates, formerly incarcerated and always using big words to impress others, while finding himself lost in his own thoughts.

You know, financial advisors are not much different than this *In Living Color* character. They use big words to illustrate relatively simple concepts. Let me break down a few to you:

Assets, Liabilities, and Net Worth. These terms are thrown around to measure not only our financial worth but our worth on this earth as well. It cannot be anything further from that. Assets are simply what you own. Liabilities are simply what you owe. Net worth is the difference between what you own and what you owe.

You can own an asset (like a house) and also have a liability (like a mortgage). Your net worth in that house is the difference between what is worth and what you still owe (also known as equity).

Diversification. This term is used often to describe the ideal portfolio of investment assets. It simply means to spread around your risks. It is what your grandmother told you – don't put all your eggs in one basket. If that basket falls, you break all your eggs. Likewise, do not invest all your assets in one stock or one asset class.

Yield. You hear this when talking about the worth of an investment, its annual yield. This simply means what you can reasonably expect to earn after owning this investment for one year. Be mindful that this annual yield will be calculated assuming compounding interest and favorable assumptions.

Volatility. This word can scare potential investors away, and it should not. Volatility is the unpredictability of the investment. In other words, you are willing to take a bigger risk on whether the investment will rise or fall. And yes, the advice you received as a child still applies – the bigger the risk, the bigger the reward.

There are many other words that sound good when spoken from a podium or an infomercial intended to impress you enough to send money. You can easily find the layman's terms' definitions of such words by relying on a basic internet search. If the first and second search results leaves you scratching your head, then move onto the third and fourth search results. Student, learn to teach thyself. If you really, really want to understand it – you will eventually find it.

What's under the hood

I have been driving cars since I was 16 years old. (14 years old if you count the time I 'borrowed' my aunt's Black Camaro – but I got in serious trouble for that stunt so I will stick with age 16). I know how to check the oil, change a tire, add air to a tire, replace windshield wipers, pump gas, and respond to a check engine light by calling my uncle. Besides those things, I know nothing about cars. Yet, I drive my car nearly every day. Investments don't work like that.

If you are going to work towards achieving financial health, you will need to become an investor. To become an investor, you will need to understand how investments work. So let's talk about the basic types of investments and how they make money.

First, let me offer my definition of investments. There are savings and investing. You should only save for things that have a specific purpose and a specific end date. For example, saving for a vacation. You need to know approximately how much you plan to spend on your dream vacation to Rome, Italy next year and then create a plan to save enough money to buy your plane ticket in February, renew your passport in April, replenish your wardrobe in August, and cover your lodging, meals, excursions, and gifts in September. In this example, you are saving money (account goes up) and spending money (account goes down). The goal should be short-term in nature – anywhere from 3 months to 3 years.

The only exception to specificity for savings is your 3-9 month emergency fund. You do not know when you will need that – and hopefully it sits idle for months and months. Even still, you need to set an amount and ensure that you have that amount in your account. When (not if) an emergency comes, you take the $800 and replace your broken dishwasher. Then you reprioritize your monthly income to ensure that you replenish the $800 you spent on that last emergency.

Investments are mechanisms to make your money work for you. The hope is that this money will grow exponentially (compounding) while waiting for your goal date to arrive. Investments are for goals that are more than 3 years. Retirement, college savings for your children and grandchildren, the dream vacation after graduating from medical school (assuming you are still in undergrad), building your down payment for your first or second home.

Investments require acceptance of risks. If your goal is less than 3 years, you do not have enough time to take large enough risks to generate large enough returns. (I am taking luck and timing out of this conversation – they do not belong in investing conversations).

Here are are some basic investments:

Stocks – Stocks represent ownership in a company. If you opened up your own auto mechanic shop you would own 100% of the stock or shares of that company. If you opened with a partner and you both equally contributed to the business then you would own 50% of the shares of that company. You could then sell half of your ownership (or 25%) to someone else. Then you would own 25% of the shares, the other person would own 25% of the shares, and your original partner would own 50% of the shares.

There are two ways to make money on owning stock. One is through dividends – this is when the owners of the company (or for a publicly-traded company, the board of directors who are elected by the owners) decide to take a portion of the profits and return it to the owners. Another way to earn money is to sell the shares for more than you bought them. This is how most people make money from stock. They buy stock when the price is low, then wait for the stock to rise in perceived value. At that point, others will want to buy the stock also – more buyers and fewer sellers lead to an increase in the price of the shares. Note, this increase in perceived value may or may not be related to the fundamentals of the company. Conversely, when the price is low and it goes lower, then others will also want to sell – more sellers and fewer buyers lead to a decrease in the price of the shares. Note, this decrease in perceived value may or may not be related to the fundamentals of the company.

Bonds – Bonds represent debt to a company or government. You agree to pool your money with other investors to make loans to an entity. The entity will initiate the ask for the loan and offer to pay a certain interest percentage each year, plus the entire balance of the loan at the end of a certain time period. The investor then can decide to keep the loan or sell it to another investor.

There are several reasons why someone would want to sell the loan to another investor. One reason is they need the money now. They initially were comfortable waiting 10 years for their money to be returned, but decided after 4 years that they need the money now. There are several reasons why someone would want to buy the loan from another investor. One reason is the interest rate offered is more attractive than the expectation of earning money from the stock market. For example, if the bond is offering a 4% return and the stock market is predicted to decline over the next two years – I'd rather take the 4% interest. This latter scenario results in the bonds being sold at a premium, or more than the amount that will be returned at the end of the loan period. Conversely, if the bond is offering a 4% return and the stock market is predicted to increase over the next two years – I'd rather invest in the stock market. These scenarios result in the bonds being sold at a discount, or less than the amount that will be returned at the end of the loan period.

Derivatives – Derivatives are contracts that aim to predict other investments. One common derivative is a stock option. An option is a contract that allows someone to purchase a stock at a specific price for a specific time period in the future. Let's say Company X's stock is currently trading at $8. A stock option is a contract that allows you to buy stock in Company X for $8 anytime over the next 4 months. (Remember you own the contract to buy the stock, not the stock itself.). If you think the stock is going to increase, you would want to buy that contract. Three month later when the stock is trading at $12, you can exercise that option and buy the stock at $8 and immediately sell it at $12. You just made money without even owning the stock or carrying the risk of the stock not performing well. Your only risk was whether that contract would be worthless in 4 months because the stock price was less than $8. In that instance, of course you would not exercise your contractual right to buy the stock at $8. The only loss you have is the cost of purchasing the contract.

Conversely if you expect the price of Company X stock to go down, you can purchase a contract that allows you to sell the stock for $8 anytime over the next 4 months. Three months later when the stock is trading at $3, you can buy the shares at $3 and then immediately sell them for $8. You just made money without even owning the stock or carrying the risk of the stock not performing well. Your only risk was whether the contract would be worthless in 4 months because the stock price was worth more than $8. In that instance, of course you would not exercise your contractual right to buy the stock at $8. The only loss you have is the cost of purchasing the contract.

Want to learn more? Let me introduce you to my friend – the internet. Very smart, but also easily distracted – so when you ask your question be specific and don't take the first answer she gives you.

What car are you driving?

The other important concept to consider is what vehicle are you using to invest? There are several, but I will focus on two: pre-tax vehicles and post-tax vehicles. It does not matter which vehicle you are driving. You can generally invest in stocks, bonds, or derivatives.

Pre-tax vehicles are the sweetest deal. You are allowed to earn money through investing while deferring the tax. At the time of this writing, the tax rate on short-term capital gains is taxed at your ordinary income tax bracket which could be anywhere from 10% to as high as 37%. Long-term capital gain tax rate is 0%, 15% or 20%, depending on your income. The treatment of short-term versus long-term depends on how long you hold the investment – more than one year is considered long-term.

Regardless of whatever tax bracket you are in – a tax-deferred investment results in at least an additional 10% of your investment income not being taxed (yet) and therefore able to participate in the power of compounding. The most common pre-tax investment vehicle is a 401k retirement account. There are also 529 College Investment Saving plans, Individual Retirement Accounts, and Thrift Savings Plans.

There are two sides to every coin. With pre-tax vehicles, you are agreeing to get in that vehicle and not get out until something happens (you retire, you turn 59½, your child goes to college, etc.). If you choose to take the money earned out of the vehicle sooner or for other purposes, there will be taxes imposed and possibly even penalties.

Post-tax vehicles do not have those same restrictions, or those same benefits. A post-tax vehicle is your run-of-the-mill brokerage account (or your fancy gamified brokerage account like Robinhood). In either case, you are investing with money that has already been taxed and any money you earn will be taxed again.

I am intentionally not showing you all the goods in this chapter, because I want you to be empowered and interested enough to learn more on your own. Anytime I am given the opportunity to present the Word of God in a church setting, I always tell the parishioners to not believe a word I say – but confirm for themselves in the Holy Bible. I offer you that same caution. Look it up for yourself.

One last thing. I am not offering investment advice.

Epilogue

The famed author Toni Morrison once said "If there is a book that you want to read, but it hasn't been written yet, you must be the one to write it". Mrs. Morrison, I heeded your advice.

I have spent nearly 35 years searching for balance in my being, perfection in my purpose, and peace in my presence. I found the three tenets of being physically stable, spiritually grounded, and financially sound as critical to living in my truth.

It is confounding how difficult life is because we see people living it every day. Intertwined with the memorable anecdotes from my own experiences are the six simple strategies which can guarantee a healthy lifestyle.

When my daughter was a teenager and my son was an adolescent, I asked them to write down their goals and then I taped it onto the ceiling above their beds. I told them I wanted their dreams articulated in their own words to be the last thing they saw at night. Those papers stayed taped to the ceiling for years – I finally removed them when I moved out of that condominium.

My daughter's goal was simple: "be happy". My son's goal was more specific: "be an accountant". Today, over 10 years later, my daughter self-describes herself as "happy" and my son is launching his first career as "an accountant". I will attribute their success in achieving their goals, in part, to them making that a constant mantra they saw every night before going to sleep.

I encourage you to write down the six strategies to healthy living. Place them on your bathroom mirror, on the dashboard of your car, on the wall near your work computer, or on the ceiling above your bed. You can interpret these strategies in your own words:

1. Do it First
2. Forgive Yourself
3. Be Consistent
4. Reduce Distractions
5. Start Small and Gradually Increase
6. Educate Yourself

I appreciate your support, and I pray you appreciate my support in building your healthy lifestyle: physically, spiritually, and financially.

About the Author

Erick O. Bell is a tenured professor of Accounting and Personal Financial Planning at Las Positas College in California. He is a Certified Public Accountant, and spent the first 15 years of his professional career serving audit and forensic clients at KPMG LLP and Deloitte LLP. Erick serves as the Chairman of the Board for the Accounting Career Awareness Program in San Francisco. His greatest accomplishment is being the father of his four accomplished children: Kasani, Mekhi, Lucas, and Benjamin; a husband to his wife, Lauren; a son to his mom and dad, Gwen and Stephen; a brother to his siblings, James, Kevin, Carlotta, Jahati, Anastasia, Zenobia, and Jamela; an uncle to his nieces and nephews, Amira, Monae, Dakari and Malulani; a cousin to all of his cousins; and a devoted church member to his pastors, Bishop Reems, Pastor Brondon and Pastor Maria.

Made in the USA
Middletown, DE
02 October 2022

11696302R00096